D0918058

THE EXISTENTIALISM OF
MIGUEL DE UNAMUNO
by *José Huertas-Jourda*

University of Florida Monographs

HUMANITIES
No. 13, Spring 1963

UNIVERSITY OF FLORIDA PRESS / GAINESVILLE, FLORIDA

This Volume is Dedicated

TO MY PARENTS

ACKNOWLEDGMENTS

The present work was presented as a thesis in partial fulfillment of the requirements for the degree of Master of Arts in Philosophy at New York University.

I wish to take this opportunity to express my deep appreciation to the members of the New York University Philosophy Department, and particularly to Professor Sidney Hook, who suggested the topic, and to Professor William Barrett, who guided the actual work. I alone am answerable for the results, but they deserve the credit for any good ideas which I have here appropriated and used.

I should like to thank also Mrs. Helen Lane and Mr. Fleming Vinson for their invaluable help in tidying up the manuscript.

José Huertas-Jourda

220603

UNIVERSITY OF FLORIDA MONOGRAPHS

HUMANITIES

CONTENTS

INTRODUCTION

The thought of Don Miguel de Unamuno is doubly inaccessible to the English reader; first, the paucity of available translations presents a quasi-insurmountable barrier to anyone who reads nothing but English; second, the peculiarities of Unamuno's method of exposition render acquaintance with only one or two of his works insufficient for an adequate understanding of his thought. In the light of this, the lack of even a good outline of the scope and depth of this thought in English philosophical literature constitutes an important lacuna. It is in order to fill this lacuna that the present thesis was written. Its purpose is one of description only. In it, it is attempted to present the framework underlying, as it were, Unamuno's celebrated contradictions. The gratuitous affirmations[1]* of the man who confesses to have tried to veil rather than reveal his thought[2] are taken and grouped by subject matter and thus are shown to constitute a rather coherent whole having definite empirical bases. The method used is similar to that developed by the students of ancient philosophy reconstituting a doctrine from fragments of thoughts dispersed in other texts. The "framework" thus obtained develops effortlessly from a critique of the means of knowledge to the elaboration of a criterion of truth, the exposition of a theory of knowledge, the description of the universe as seen by someone believing in such a theory and, finally, the elaboration of an ethic compatible with these criteria of knowledge.

Such an outline is necessarily sketchy, but it does represent a necessary work prefacing any critical study of Unamuno's thought so long as his writings remain generally unavailable to the English reader. Critique and description seemed incompatible in a study designed to present rather than either buttress or weaken a highly personal and fresh philosophical outlook. It appeared at this point preferable to let the texts speak as clearly as they could by themselves without injecting any other clarification than that immediately obvious from them. While no claim is made that all obscurities are Unamuno's, it is asserted that no special effort was made to be more Unamunian than Unamuno.

The texts used were the Spanish ones and except when otherwise specified were contained in the published volumes of the *Complete Works*. Reference to this edition will be made as follows: Unamuno,

*Notes begin on page 61.

1

OC, the volume number in Roman numerals, the page number, the title of the work quoted. The only other abbreviation will be *Del Sentimiento,* instead of *Del Sentimiento Trágico de la Vida en los Hombres y en los Pueblos.* All translations are mine.

Before considering the thought, however, a word about the man. Miguel de Unamuno, born in Bilbao, Biscay, Spain, on September 29, 1864,[3] died in Salamanca, Leon, Spain, the 31st of December, 1936, in the late afternoon;[4] between these two dates spans as flamboyant a lived adventure as was ever given to a philosopher. Playwright, novelist, essayist, pamphleteer, philosopher, poet, professor of Greek and of linguistics, as well as, successively, Rector of the University of Salamanca, political exile, Rector for Life of Salamanca, Citizen of Honor of the Spanish Republic, and political prisoner under surveillance in Salamanca: thus could the manifold career of the greatest Don Miguel since Cervantes be sketchily summarized, and though some of its magnitude might perchance be imparted, the greatness that moved men like Salvador de Madariaga to call him "the living symbol of his nation and of his time"[5] would not be expressed.

For the greatness and the strength of Unamuno do not reside in the itemized list of his actions. It is, in a sense, minor that he should have defied the King of Spain and General Primo de Rivera. Minor also the fact that he should have won and that his return to Spain should have coincided with the departure of the King. Even though the interview with the King in 1922 and Unamuno's refusal to relent, Unamuno's opposition after the coup d'etat of 1923, his exile to Fuerteventura and his subsequent escape to France acquire "titanic" and even "world"[6] dimensions, taking, with Unamuno's victory, the aspect of a fight between a David and a Goliath, this is not where the true greatness of the man resides. Indeed, the events of 1936, his endorsement of the rebels and his public rejection of their aims and methods later on, followed by the revocation by the rebel authorities of his rectorship and his enforced silence under surveillance,[7] and, after this public death by which the voice that had sometimes guided, often irritated, always prodded Spain practically daily since the 1890's, was stilled; after this, his physical death some months later, all these events suddenly reveal— in the silence and the emptiness left by the political leader whose historical remains will clutter the mind of historians with a few dates and gestures—the presence of the thinker, the weight of the man whose imprint was hewn, not merely into the history of his nation, but primarily into its thought.

2

To those who, as Pío Baroja is reported to have said, expected to see, after his death, his work "disintegrate," bereft of "the powerful arm which supported the frame,"[8] can be opposed those who see in the political activity of Unamuno his "great sin."[9] Neither are correct. The greatness of Unamuno resides in the fact that he cannot be summarized or explained away by his political actions, but that they form an integral part of his thought. Unamuno as a political figure teaches in much the same way as Gandhi taught, and in the same way his actions have both an immediate and a transcendent meaning. It is this transcendent meaning, this "eternal presence" as a teacher to any and all, anywhere, which truly reveals the formidable stature of the man. Others have overthrown kings, others have patiently suffered exile alleviating their anguish by writing barbed pamphlets against their tormentors, few have transcended their historical circumstances into a timeless spring of wisdom and solace, few have been able to acquire, in spite of their activity, a new presence.

This is not to say that this new presence is not disputed. It would be out of character with Unamuno if his works and his thought should become universally recognized and praised. Although some historians of philosophy pretend to have some doubts as to the *bien fondé* of any inclusion of Unamuno's name in their Parnassus,[10] these doubts can be ascribed more to prejudice and misunderstanding than to any real philosophical grounds. Increasingly, however, recognition in the form of at least serious criticism[11] or even careful consideration,[12] is coming to Unamuno. And the historians only follow an array of scholarly works such as, for example, François Meyer's *L'Ontologie de Miguel de Unamuno*,[13] or P. M. Oromi's *Pensamiento Filosófico de M. de Unamuno*,[14] who generally concur with Ramón Ceñal Lorente[15] in recognizing the heterodox character of Unamuno's philosophical contribution while perhaps claiming, as J. Kessel is reported by F. Meyer to have done,[16] that there is in the Unamunian "incoherence" "eine bewusste Systemlosigkeit."

It is this "bewusste Systemlosigkeit" which is the problem and perhaps the key to Unamuno's thought. Unamuno himself time and again claimed that all his works were but the development of "a unique and same fundamental thought which you see unrolling itself in multiple forms"[17] and that the "intimate contradictions" were "at least apparent,"[18] mischievously warning the reader not to look for "coherent things."[19] And yet, this is the man who, in the words of one of his detractors, "has been a genial guesser and anticipator of many im-

3

portant discoveries with respect to the reality that life is, and remains an effective precursor of the metaphysics of existence or of human life."[20] This is the man who, as remarks a foreign observer, has gone on influencing each coming Spanish generation more than the preceding one, being now closer to the present one than his "rival," José Ortega y Gasset.[21] Surely, such a presence deserves study.

Unamuno is, still today, "the most representative and the most profound writer of the generation of '98,"[22] this marked promotion of men coming of age in a decadent, defeated land to take their place upon a battlefield bloodied in many an open civil war and poisoned by the constant infringement of the governing upon the liberties of the governed. The defeat of Spain at the hands of the United States, an upstart as nations go, showed to all conclusively that the other party, by preventing its opponent from ruling, was bringing the country to ruin. The generation which then arose "adopted a critical attitude towards the Spanish National Problem,"[22] that is to say that it rejected slogans and parties and put them all under its critical glare. Unamuno, as the oldest and by far the ablest member, contributed all he could to this movement. He went further than any of his cohorts: just as Homer presented the Trojan War through the keyhole of Achilles' anger, Unamuno saw, through the problems of Spain, the problems of man and transcended the former to the latter. There is no facet of human life and concern that he has not in some way touched. There is no problem with which he was concerned on which he did not make a significant comment worthy of note and debate.

1. UNAMUNO'S THEORY
OF LANGUAGE

According to Miguel de Unamuno, language is the main tool of knowledge, all knowledge is linguistic in nature, and all attempts to know must be attempts to formulate in a language of some kind that which is to be known.[1] There are different kinds of languages: the language common to the members of an ethnic group, and the technical languages used by different sciences.[2] Although the technical languages are designed to replace the common one in a specific area of endeavor,[3] it is, in fact, the elaboration of the common language which made their elaboration possible,[4] and therefore, the common language must be considered fundamental.[5]

This language is a "social thing."[6] It is the depository of the experiences of the men who have elaborated it, and their creation.[7] In it they have put their "abstract conception of the world and of life";[8] its roots "carry in their metaphorical strength a whole content of impure experience, of human social experience."[9] And this content is the composite product of the effort of each, for "each one of us starts, in order to think, knowingly or not, willingly or not, from what the others who preceded him and are around him have thought."[10] "Thought rests in prejudgments and the prejudgments go in the language."[11]

The common language stems from the necessity to "transmit our thoughts to our neighbors."[12] The first word of the first language was elaborated in turn by the man who thought and spoke it, and by the man to whom he said it. Both the speaker and the listener "created" the word: "the word is creation."[13]

Much of what Unamuno has to say about ideas can be attributed to words as well, as a special case of an idea represented by one word, since: "With the word, like God, the man/forges and carves his reality of ideas."[14] As a matter of fact, Unamuno never bothers to make precise whether he is speaking about ideas as embodied in the word or as embodied in the expression. Thus when he notes that "the common language, in effect, is that of common sense, formed by the practical necessities of life and directed to their service,"[15] he seems to be talking about words only. However, when he affirms that "common sense operates with commonplaces,"[16] adding, "And there are cadavers of ideas . . . or commonplaces,"[16] he seems to be talking about anything from a word to a commonly held belief. At this stage, it is only necessary to take his remarks as concerning words singly.

Consequently, though the word is the depository of even private human experience, when a word has become commonplace and its meaning is readily understood by all, the contribution of our own private experience to its evolution may become so slight as to be quite negligible. The words applicable to our daily routine become themselves so adapted to the experience they symbolize that no amount of work is required any more on the part of either the speaker or the listener. This, in fact, is not a situation peculiar to our daily routine, as the ambiguous usage of the word idea indicates, it is a situation peculiar to any habitual usage of any term between as wide or as restricted a linguistic community as the case may be. "Ideas, like money, are, in effect, in the last instance nothing more than representations of riches and instruments of exchange, until such time as, when they have given us a logical common denominator, we exchange directly our states of consciousness."[17] Habitual usage of terms produces a kind of fossilization of their meaning which enables each user to communicate readily with any other member of that particular linguistic community.

But, as Unamuno time and again intimates,[18] such ready communication does not do justice to the richness of the word. And he distinguishes between what he calls the "concrete word,"[19] the "word of doing,"[20] and what he terms the "dead idea,"[21] the "word of saying."[20]

The concrete word is the symbol used in the full perception of its uniqueness and richness, in its emotional dimension as well as in its intellectual one.[22] It is the word used as an approximation of the experience it is meant to relate, in which the experience always overflows the word, and the area of coincidence between the meaning meant and the meaning transmitted is always smaller than the area of the meaning experienced, "because this dead paper on which I write neither shouts, nor shrieks, nor sighs, nor weeps, because language was not meant so that you and I could understand each other."[23]

As against this, the term used abstractly is not meant to contain any private experience; it is no more than the residue of the experiences of others, and it is handled quite detachedly, no matter what it says. It is handled "intellectually"[24] only. The possibility to use terms in this detached way comes from the inertia of language. "As soon as a thought of ours remains frozen by writing, expressed, crystallized, it already remains dead,"[25] and upon the "corpse of the expression, its words,"[26] dictionaries and grammars are made[26] and the words tend to remain upon the

6

ground, conquered, without further development or deepening of their meaning.

Even that conquered ground, however, is not devoid of riches: it is the sediment of other experiences, and, for the person who wishes to consider it as such and to delve into its treasures, it may be the source of similar experiences. The words "begin to be a living body when a soul animates them."[26] It must be noted, however, that Unamuno does not explicitly state that words can be taken in a totally detached manner. Although he does not specify whether he considers it to be the case only when the words are felt as well as said or thought, he does consider them "dynamogenic" in the same way that colors are said to be so, writing:

> If one man were constantly encircled by a red lamp and another by a blue lamp, and they could communicate with each other, it is clear that they would fall in agreement with each other with respect to the color of things, and both would call each color with the same name, since all the colors would transform themselves in coordination, and perchance these men would believe that they see the world in the same way. Their respective positions with respect to the vision of colors—because they would each be absolute—would erase all differences. But colors are not the only elements of vision, the light of each of them influences the organism chemically, and each one in a distinct manner, the red being the most *dynamogenic* color, or that excites the organism, and the blue depresses it. And thus, even though the two men of the hypothesis would correspond in their mode of explication of the world, their vital energy would become modified in a most distinct manner. The sentence: "vanity of vanities and all vanity" is a blue sentence, and that of: "plenitude of plenitudes and all plenitude" is a red one.[27]

Questions might be raised about the possibility of these two men agreeing as to the respective colors of the things in their universe; however, the two important points are, first, that they see the same thing differently but do not realize that there is a difference; second, that although they cannot objectively pinpoint the difference, subjectively, unconsciously even, they feel it and express it in their different energy levels. Those two points are central to Unamuno's conception of language.

For Unamuno, men only suppose that they want to say the same things when they use the same words, and Don Quixote, his spokesman, "knew that with the same words we are accustomed to say opposed

7

things, and with opposed words the same thing. Thanks to which we can converse and understand ourselves."[28] In other words, much as the two men and their lights, each person experiences the world in a different way, but "if all the representations are different, they are all translations of a unique original, all reduce to unity, for otherwise men would not understand each other, and this fundamental unity of the distinct human representations is what makes language possible."[29]

The willful rashness of these affirmations should not lure anyone into an equally sweeping rejection. Unamuno is trying to bring to attention as forcefully as he can that words are mere shadows of what they are purported to convey because they leave the most important item out— the emotional factor: "You can give me the tone and the intensity with which in you the world vibrates, the note which in your heart resounds; but you cannot give me the timbre with which you receive it, which is your own timbre. And if you transmit it to me, it is through an esthetic emotion, it is through a work of art!"[30]

Consequently, the proper use of language is the one in which it is recognized that we experience the words here and now, endowing them with the residue of our own experience, and in which an attempt is made to do justice to that experience. Language was not made, it is being made, here and now. To think that words can be used with only their common sense is worse than an error of fact, it is an unwarranted assumption. Just as a word cannot be used entirely subjectively, since language is a "social thing," it cannot be used completely abstractly either, it is "dynamogenic."

Unamuno's analysis of language led him, therefore, to the recognition of two antagonistic aspects which coexist in the word: the dead residue of the written word, and the evolving meaning of the experienced word; each of these aspects presupposes the other, neither could exist separately, yet one is the negation of the other.

This inherent ambiguity once recognized and accepted, it is no longer possible to consider constant successful use of a term as an understanding of its meaning in its totality. The most familiar word may contain notions peculiar to the linguistic community which uses it. Likewise, another community's language may, by contradistinction, both present us with new notions and reveal to us hitherto unnoticed aspects of our own tongue. "He who knows only his own tongue does not even know that. Man only reflects upon what is his own by putting it in comparison with the alien."[31] Really to experience a word, therefore, one must be able not only to use it but also to compare it.

Furthermore, the term has had a development within its own linguistic community. This history of the term as contained in its etymology is revelatory in the same way as the comparison with a foreign tongue may be. "Each people has gone on setting down in its language its abstract conception of the world and of life, and in the extension and comprehension that it gives to each word is implicit its philosophy."[32] To experience a term properly is, therefore, to delve into its etymological history. And Unamuno time and again insists upon this, affirming, "A language, in effect, is a potential philosophy," and claiming, "The philosopher does no other thing but to take out of the language what all the people have put in it throughout centuries."[33]

To use a word properly is an altogether different problem since, instead of trying to fit our experience to the idea contained in it, we must try to make it fit our experience. The dead residue becomes the negative aspect which must be fought. Whenever Unamuno uses the term "idea" pejoratively, he refers to an expression in which that inert residue is not fought, and to him that means mental laziness and lack of originality. Though the common sense has its use—"The common language, in effect, is that of common sense, formed by the practical necessities of life and directed to their service"[34]—its field is "the collective, the common," not "the individual, the proper."[34] It may give us ready-made ideas, and indeed it does, but "thoughts must be made."[35] "The thought is limited by the word,"[36] not completely embodied by it. Thus, if the thing to do with ideas is to break them in, "like boots,"[37] the thing to do with thoughts is to express them in spite of the language. "And what we call paradox is the most effective corrective of the crudenesses and platitudes of common sense. The paradox is what opposes itself most to common sense."[38] It is "the most genuine product of the proper sense."[38] And the proper sense, "the scarcest of all the senses,"[39] is properly the appanage of the one "who has style, the one who is himself, the one who exists,"[39] that is to say, the one who does not hesitate to bend words to his necessity, even at the cost of speaking or writing in paradoxes.

Unamuno's defense of the paradox is a major tenet of his thought; for him, the paradox is invaluable on at least two counts: it is "the most effective element of progress,"[40] since it enables the individual to express a meaning hitherto unexpressed, and it is "the most vivid and most effective manner to transmit the truth,"[41] presumably, in that it demands thought and attention on the part of the reader or the listener, thus forcing them to experience the idea, rather than just receive it.

9

Other means of expression preconized by Unamuno are the metaphor:[42] "language is essentially metaphorical,"[43] and verse: "verse is, without doubt, the natural language of the depth of the spirit,"[44] all equally directed against the inertia and uniformity which common sense would impose upon all, an inertia and a uniformity which Unamuno takes great pains to show illusory. To Unamuno, "Common sense belongs to no one, it is not the property of anyone, it is ownerless and resists monopolies."[45] No one, therefore, can claim to know common sense with any certainty.[46] Anyone avowedly committed to a strict obedience of common sense is an "idiot"[47] if all he does in fact possess is common sense, if he "lacks his own sense."[47] The meaning of terms evolves, albeit slowly, and this is a cardinal fact which Unamuno does not want overlooked. For him, "Change is always of individual origin,"[48] that is to say, the product of proper sense, and the inevitability of change must be taken into account. Not the least damning factor in his eyes is that, to the partisans of unmitigated common sense, "every new scientific truth must appear as a paradox,"[48] though the paradox is only, after all, "the commonplace of tomorrow."[49]

Unamuno confronts us, therefore, with a conception of language in which he cleaves the word into two antagonistic aspects, neither of which can be completely discarded in favor of the other. If the emphasis is put upon the fossilized aspect, the word is used according to its presumed "common" sense; if it is put on the other, the word is used concretely, according to a "proper" sense, toward the understanding of which anyone interested has to work according to his own lights and without much of a certainty of corroboration from any consensus, since it is all primarily a matter of private experience and approximation.

The special case of the development of the scientific technical languages furnishes Unamuno with a good example of both the aptness of his analysis and the importance of the "private" aspect of the word:

> One of the major advantages of the use of Greek in scientific technical terminology is that, as the words *are in Greek*, they do not act as an anchor which binds the idea to its first form, impeding its development. The noun *esthetics* is applied today to an idea which does not correspond to the original one, and it is indubitable that if the *psycho* of *psychology* would evoke in our mind, spontaneously and immediately, ideas as vivid, deep rooted, and tenacious as those evoked by the noun *soul*, psychology would have lost part of its progress. In the noun, which is their flesh, the concepts bear the stain of original sin.[50]

10

Science, while emphasizing the fixed aspect of the word as much as possible, indirectly offers a recognition of their experiential content since the scientists would rather coin a new word than redefine an old one.

Such a conception of language as this raises a number of problems, the least of which is not that of truth. Related to it is the problem of interpretation of texts. On this Unamuno was categorical. In an essay entitled, "Upon the Reading and Interpretation of the 'Quixote'," he asks: "What Cervantes wanted to say in his Quixote, if he wanted to say anything, what does that have to do with what it occurs to us, the others, to see in it?"[51] a rhetorical question tantamount to an affirmation of the exclusive superiority of subjectivity in this matter.

His analysis of language, which forced him to abandon the guide of common sense as the sole criterion of the adequacy of terms, forces Unamuno to delve into the problem of truth. The question that must be answered is twofold: can anyone meaningfully use the terms "true" and "false" with respect to statements made by himself, and if so, what does it mean; can anyone meaningfully use the terms "true" and "false" with respect to statements made by others, and if so, what does it mean.

2. THE "QUIXOTIC" THEORY OF TRUTH

"One never dreams twice the same dream,"[1] says the protagonist in one of Unamuno's novels to his author. In the same Heraclitean vein, Unamuno tirelessly stresses that the same experience never recurs, that no idea is ever experienced twice in the same way, for "there is nothing which is the same in two successive moments of its being."[2]

In such a context of flux and absolute individuality, any criterion of truth depending upon some sort of objective corroboration is in fact useless. All there is is the uniqueness of the experience now lived. If this is not the experience of a word, all that can be done is to salvage it partially from oblivion by symbolizing it, however imperfectly, with the rough tools others have forged for us and which, in turn, we forge. If it is the experience of a word, or an idea, it can never be claimed to be the very same as that of any other person experiencing the same word, or the same idea.

The only qualified judge, therefore, is the person who is doing the experiencing here and now. If he believes the expression to fit the experience, or if he believes the experience to fit the expression, then they are true to him: "Things are all the more true as they are more believed,"[3] and, "the truth, ordinarily, is completely individual, personal, and incommunicable."[4] "The truth is that which, moving us to act in one way or another, would cause our result to cover our aim."[5]

The use of the conditional mood in this last sentence is especially important: Unamuno hereby stresses the primacy of the present belief over the future result. The truth is what moves us now, what lures us to act, what seems to us to be the thing to do, that is to say, the thing to be done, the aim to be sought. Whether "our result covers our aim" is, as the use of the conditional indicates, a secondary matter; what is important is what is believed now, or in Unamuno's terms, what is lived now, for "life is the criterion of truth, and not logical concordance."[5]

To compare the result with the belief is a matter of logical concordance: the logical concordance between two residues of experience, two dead ideas; it has no bearing upon the truth of the unique experiences of which they are the imperfect trace—"the idea is an epiphenomenon, a reflection, a mere shadow."[6] As against this, "Truth is what is believed with the whole heart and with the whole soul. And what

12

is it to believe something wholeheartedly and with the whole soul? To act accordingly."[7] Not the result, but the present action of the person who now proclaims a certain belief, is the criterion of its truth. And the contrary to truth is not error, but lie: "He who teaches one of those things that they call truths without believing it, lies."[8]

It is difficult, at first, to associate such an idea of truth with any linguistic expression. The reason for this is perhaps that the sign with fixed definition upon which grammars and dictionaries are elaborated dwarfs the importance of the experiential content which Unamuno wishes to emphasize. He wishes us to deal, not with that fixed entity, but with the slice of life each sign labels, however inadequately. In the "concrete" language, either the experience becomes expression, or the expression becomes experience, and in either case to experience is to give to a sign that which it does not have on its own, namely, life. For "there are dead truths and live truths, or better said, since the truth cannot die nor be dead, there are people who receive certain truths as a dead thing, purely theoretical, and which in no manner vivifies their spirit,"[9] which in no way moves them to act. For Unamuno these people are liars, and the lie "is that which kills":[10] "it stifles noble impulses"[11] (it leaves unexpressed the experience in fact lived, thus condemning it to oblivion, killing it), "and aborts sterile monsters"[11] (it leaves the ideas it pretends to endorse unexperienced, thus leaving them as the "cadavers of thought" they are when they are not lived)..

In this world, therefore, "all is truth and all is lie,"[11] depending upon the way in which anything is believed by anyone, and "every belief which leads to works of life is a true (in the sense of genuine) belief, and it is a pretense when it leads to works of death."[12] "You know Pythagoras' Theorem and there comes a case in which your life depends upon the discovery of a square having an area three times as big as another, and you don't know how to use such a theorem? . . . It is not true for you."[13] To know is to be able to use what it is that we believe we know: to believe to know is to attempt to use what it is that we believe to know; "he who believes, believes in what will come, that is, in what he hopes. No one believes, strictly speaking, that which is or that which has been, if not as guarantee, as substance of what will be."[14]

The first part of the question asked in the preceding chapter is almost answered completely. True is that which is genuinely believed; false that which is mere pretense of belief. The individual can meaningfully use those terms with respect to the statements he makes, albeit he may be the only person qualified to know whether or not their application is

13

correct, or rather, true, since the truth is "individual, personal, and in-communicable." But that first part is only "almost" answered because what exactly constitutes belief has not as yet been made precise.

"To believe is to create,"[15] better still, "to believe is in the first instance to want to believe,"[16] but, "Be aware, nevertheless, as to how to want to believe, that is to say, to want to create is not precisely to believe or to create, although it is the beginning of both."[17] To believe is, therefore, not merely to rely upon certain ideas or to characterize certain experiences with the equanimity and the emotional detachment of an IBM machine computing a problem. It is, on the contrary, striving, in doubt and in want, as the willful use of the word *querer* indicates. *Querer* means to want as well as to cherish, in a happy ambiguity of which Unamuno makes the most; its emotional connota-tions of desire and dire need are only partially present in the English equivalent "to want."

To believe, in Unamuno's conception, is not a trivial matter; it is an emotional state in which are commingled hope, desire, and, simul-taneously, feelings of lack and of doubt. It is to be noted, however, that Unamuno's usage of the word "to believe," does not always conform to the above interpretation. However, by bearing in mind that in this context he wishes to describe a thought process and not to use the term in its common acceptance—i.e., as equivalent to "to be reasonably sure of"—when he does use the term in its common acceptance, the proper transposition should be made. Thus, when he writes: "And to think is to doubt and nothing more than to doubt. One believes, knows, imagines without doubt; neither faith, nor knowledge, nor the imagi-nation suppose doubt and doubt even destroys them, but one cannot think without doubt. And doubt is that which of faith and of knowl-edge—which are something static, quiet, dead—makes thought, which is dynamic, unquiet, live,"[18] it is apparent that there is more similarity between his use of the term "thought" in this quotation, and his mean-ing for the term "to believe" in the previous one, than between both uses of the term "to believe."

Of this "subjective"[19] truth, Unamuno has given stronger formula-tions, calling it "the intimate participation of my soul with the Uni-versal Soul."[20] This should not be construed as incompatible with the criterion of belief and doubt given above. Such participation is more of an ultimate goal, a continuously receding aim, than a criterion. "The anguish of the soul is the door of the substantial truth. Suffer, in order to create and, believing, live. . . . The truth is what makes live, not what makes think."[21] The word "think" is here used in contradistinction with "feel," and pejoratively denotes the mere intellectual handling of ideas.

Thus, to hold something subjectively true is to give it life, and if it already has some, more. The experience, if it is believed, demands an expression, created in anguish, and as appropriate as can be; the expression, if it is believed, demands to be experienced anew, and being experienced, changed to fit the new content, in an ever-widening, never-ending cycle of creative desire. The only rule is to be sincere.[22] "That which we must flee is insincerity and falsehood. If you feel something crawling inside yourself, begging you freedom, open the stream and let it run, whatever and however it surges."[23] "There is nothing more terrible, in effect, than frivolity, superficiality, that is to say, barren-ness."[24]

Thus the first part of the question asked at the close of the previous chapter is answered: any man may use the terms "true" and "false" with respect to his private experience and be judged upon the sincerity with which he applies them. Remains the second part: "can anyone meaningfully use the terms 'true' and 'false' with respect to statements made by others, and if so, what does it mean."

Clearly, the above criterion cannot be used unless one presupposes that two interlocutors can sufficiently cohere in their usages of terms in order to understand each other even partially. In fact, in all the preceding discussion, although the inadequacy of the word to symbolize completely the experience has been stressed, the possibility of the use of the word has not been quarreled with. Unamuno continuously refers to words and the linguistic expression of thoughts. Yet the mere existence of such a mode of expression is testimonial to the existence of some sort of agreement upon their meaning and usage: "we need logic, this terrible power, in order to transmit thoughts and perceptions, and even in order to think and to perceive, because we think with words, we perceive with forms. To think is to speak with one's own self, and speech is social, and social are thought and logic."[25] If only to symbolize our own private experience, therefore, we need symbols which are not completely ruled by our mere whim; subjective truth is not enough and must be supplemented.

Unamuno is led to recognize "two classes of truth: the logical or objective, the contrary of which is the error, and the moral or subjective, to which is opposed the lie."[26]

The objective truth is "something collective, social, even civil; that

15

upon which we agree, and with which we understand each other, is true."[27] The criterion of objective truth is "coherence,"[28] and though, fundamentally, the pattern of cohesion upon which the truth of an expression is judged be the same, there are different levels of coherence, depending upon the degree of systematization of the context in which the expression is put.

The first level is that of the coherence of distinct experiences or representations which have enough points of similarity to be roughly symbolized by the same idea:

> Remember how composite photographs are made, for which various individuals of a family are taken; for example, if they are six, each of them is projected upon the plate, with the same focus and position in each case, the sixth part of the time necessary in order to obtain a clear and distinct proof. In this manner the images superimpose one another, the analogous traits, those of the family, corroborate each other, and the individual or distinct traits form around these a nimbus, a vague penumbra. The larger the number of individuals or that of analogies between them, the more marked will become the compound image, and the vaguer the nimbus; and, contrariwise, the fewer the individuals or the fewer the analogies, the more fleeting and vague the image in a nimbus that prevails. Then by taking these compound images in order to compare and to combine them the ones with the others, and to superimpose them in their turn, the concrete part of them defines itself, and much of the nimbus disappears. Every compound as it enters as a component into a unity superior to itself accentuates its individuality.[29]

Clearly, the modus operandi here described is diametrically opposed to the one preconized by Unamuno earlier. The uniqueness of the irretrievable experiences is no longer the focal point, but much to the contrary, its similitudes with others of our own, and, after proper symbolization and presumably sufficient communication, its similitudes with the experiences of others. From this first level of coherence, Unamuno is led to recognize what one might call the coherence of conformity, basis of language, common sense, and empty intellectualism.[30] Coherence, at this level, is merely servile obedience to common usage, and its major merit is to jell the meaning of terms into sufficiently static "common" senses as to allow the compilation of dictionaries and the like.

Upon these "cadavers of thoughts" science, this "cemetery of dead ideas,"[31] is built by reason. "From the reflected and full ideas, the mind soars to ideas of these ideas by abstraction."[32] "A knowledge becomes scientific as it makes itself more precise and organized, as it passes from qualitative to quantitative precision."[33] "In proportion as science, going from merely qualitative to quantitative provision, purifies itself of the vulgar conception, it strips itself little by little of the vulgar language, which only expresses qualities, in order to put on the scientific, *rational* language, which tends to express the quantitative."[33] The coherence here achieved is the coherence of systematization.[34]

Whereas subjective truth emphasized the uniqueness of the experience and demanded total sincerity in its symbolization as a goal, the goal of objective truth is identity: "Logic tends to reduce everything to identities and genera, so that each representation should have no more than one, and only one, content in any place, time or relation in which it occurs to us. . . . The identity, which is death, is the aspiration of the intellect."[35] And this identity is the identity of abstract signs equated to other abstract signs. It can never be the identity of the sign to the experience: "The mind searches the dead, since the live eludes it."[35] In that fundamental divorce lies the root of the necessity for objective truth to be coherence: since the sign cannot do justice to the experience, but only to some features of many experiences, in the coherence of the usage with previous usage, of private usage with common usage, must lie the criterion. From the grouping of experiences under a sign, to the classifying of signs into an ever more intricate systematization, the work of reason is a continuous abstraction on the pattern of the elaboration of "composite photographs."

The terms "true" and "false" can therefore meaningfully be used with respect to statements made by others, and they indicate that these statements either do, or do not, concur with "the general system of all our concepts."[36]

At this point, there are some pertinent questions which Unamuno has raised in different parts of his works, and which must be considered. The first one concerns the truth of a coherent system taken as a whole. It is one of Unamuno's strongest convictions that, although any particular part of the system can be considered as true with respect to it, inasmuch as it coheres with it, although any "concept" can be accepted or rejected on the grounds that it does or does not cohere with the whole, "with respect to the whole system, to the totality, as outside of it there is nothing known to us, it is not fitting to say whether or not it is true. It is imaginable that the Universe be in itself, outside from us, in much another manner than it seems to us, although this is a supposition which lacks all rational sense."[37] That is to say that outside the system, there

17

is nothing "rationally" known to us, and that because of this, "such a supposition lacks all rational sense," but that is not to say that it may not have another kind of "sense."

Indeed, the "system" as a whole cannot give any necessity to the Universe as a whole: "what absolute logical necessity, independent of the fact that the Universe exists, is there that there should be a Universe or any other thing?"[37] And the fact that there is such a Universe, if it is not part of the system, cannot be objectively true.

Furthermore, Unamuno insists that "science does not exist except in the personal consciousness and thanks to it; astronomy, mathematics, have no other reality than the one they hold as knowledge in the minds of those who learn and cultivate them."[38] Thus science, the "cemetery of dead ideas," must be lived and experienced; that is to say, be subjectively true, if its objective truth is to be known. The mere pious mouthing of formulae and numbers is not enough: "science is something live, always in process of formation."[39]

Finally, though the sciences may tend toward a "universal algebra,"[40] science is "before all, and above all a school of sincerity and humility. Science teaches us, in fact, to submit our reason to the truth and to know and to judge things as they are."[41] That is to say, science is directed to the knowledge of the fact, and must submit to the fact,[42] and the fact is a matter of subjective experience: "That which we call reality, objective or logical truth, is nothing but the prize conceded to sincerity, to truthfulness. To him who would be absolutely and always truthful and sincere, Nature would have no secret whatever."[43]

Thus, just as the subjective criterion of truth was found wanting in a crucial respect, so is the objective criterion of truth. In fact, both criteria require each other though one be the negation of the other, and vice versa. The ambiguity of language leads Unamuno to the recognition of a double criterion of truth composed of two mutually antagonistic parts, indissolubly commingled. This is the best that can be done, according to Unamuno, and as far as the "true truth," the "one which is independent of us . . . of this one, who knows?"[44] Unamuno certainly does not claim to do so.

The Unamunian criterion has the double merit of pointing to the human element in even the most abstruse theory (forcing all to become convinced by the strain of their own wits, and not merely by the imposition of awe), and to the social element in even the most esoteric revelation (forcing all to be satisfied only when as much of the experience as could be salvaged by expression—whatever its means—has been

18

saved, and not merely by an avowal of indigence). It has also the merit of being, not an a priori lucubration, but an empirical study. Its ambivalence is a disadvantage that should not be minimized, but as a criterion, it is the best that can be gotten, and the one with which men in fact work.

How do men work with it? This is a question best answered by a study of the means and the methods of knowledge, and one upon which Unamuno has dwelt considerably in various contexts. His views upon it need to be treated separately.

3. THE METHOD AND THE MEANS OF KNOWLEDGE

The only instance of simultaneous and equal applicability of both parts of Unamuno's criterion of truth to a knowledge occurs when an objectively true statement is being created, as, for example, when H. Poincaré, upon his return home, verifies his inspiration about a problem in mathematics.[1] Although Unamuno does not give any such example, this one seems to fit best the conditions he outlines as follows: "The idea which realizes itself is true. And it is only true inasmuch as it is realized; the realization which makes it live, gives it truth; the one which fails in the practical or theoretical reality is false, because there is also a theoretical reality. Truth is that which you make intimate and make your own; only the idea that you live is true to you."[2]

Such a situation, however, presupposes two different kinds of knowledge: first, a body of objectively true "theoretical" notions to form that "reality" of which Unamuno speaks; secondly, a genuine belief in the "idea" to prod the researcher along. Poincaré's anecdote is a case in point, since he insists upon the immediate and complete certainty he felt at the moment of inspiration. These two kinds of knowledge Unamuno characterizes as the "science of the head" and the "wisdom of the heart,"[3] in a somewhat different context. One puts the emphasis upon the objective part of the criterion of truth; the other, upon the subjective part.

The "science of the head" is the product of intelligence and reason. Reason, in Unamuno's conception, seems to be a common regulatory power; it "is a social product," "owes its origin to language," and "is social and common."[4] The intelligence seems to be a private faculty in the same way as "the sentience," or the affective powers,[5] and "the will."[6] But Unamuno sometimes uses reason as if it were a private faculty as well.[7] Possibly, the intelligence holds for Unamuno a place antecedent to that of reason, as the faculty which helped create the common language from which in turn reason arose.

The method of the intelligence and reason is "logic";[8] but the word logic, in varying contexts, is given different meanings by Unamuno. The most common is a pejorative one which denotes a popular misapplication of the adjective "logical" to whatever statement fits common prejudices.[9] Another one denotes logical systems such as the

Scholastic,[10] and still another, the inherent quality of consequence in someone's thought.[11] Last, an important use, the word logic is taken as denoting that which pertains to words, as when Unamuno speaks of the "metalogical bases" of knowledge, that is to say, of the experiential content of words.[12]

This last use, however, affords us some clarification as to what Unamuno meant by logic as a method. To him, the logic which "tends to reduce all to identities and to genera,"[13] is the very method of abstraction which makes language possible in the first place. By trying to reduce "every representation until each has no more than one and the same content in any place, time or relation in which it occurs to us,"[14] it, in fact, separates the sign from the original experience, and proceeds to relate signs to signs, independently of their content.

The main characteristic of the knowledge afforded by the intelligence and reason, through the use of logic, is, therefore, relation. "The rational, in fact, is nothing but the relational."[13] "Forms fitting one into the other and forms of these forms in an unending process is the world of science,"[14] and these forms are as detached from the concreteness of the experience or the thing as reason can make them, striving toward the Hegelian ideal of the "supreme form,"[14] "this dream of the Quixote of philosophy."[14]

Thus reason explains the world and existence,[15] but it does so by the description of a process: "The doctrine of evolution has resulted in that each moment be considered as a point in a process from which it finds its justification, each fact as a product, and in that the explanation of things be sought in their genesis."[16] Every thing, every fact is dissolved in a set of causes, or relations: "reason limits itself to the relation of irrational things. Mathematics is the only perfect science, inasmuch as it adds, subtracts, multiplies and divides numbers, but not real things of volume; it is the most formal of the sciences."[17]

For Unamuno, therefore, the "intelligence does not need anything outside of itself in which to take exercise; it founds itself with the ideas themselves,"[18] and operates best with ideas alone, as in mathematics: the necessity to explain the world is foreign to it, and its explanation of it is set upon a plane removed from the world as it is experienced. The "science of the head" reveals to us a world of appearances;[19] logic "administers the apparent relations of things";[20] this knowledge is "the reflection of the Universe in the mind,"[20] but only a reflection, because it is detached from the continuous flow of change and life. But this is not to say that this "reflection" has no use; on the contrary.

21

Unamuno believes firmly in science, as a discipline, and as a necessary part of human knowledge: "Understanding the world, reducing it to a vivid ideal representation, not only does one create a world within one's own self, reflection of the exterior world, but with the former the latter is dominated. Science dominates strength, an old truth that will never be enough meditated."[21]

Objective knowledge is bound to "the necessity to live and to gather nourishment in order to succeed in doing so."[22] From the barest necessity, and when the means to satisfy it have become so efficient that time is left for other things, stems "this other that we could call superfluous knowledge,"[22] science, which remains nevertheless, mostly a matter of "economy"[23] of thought and effort. Science "satisfies increasingly our increasing logical or mental necessities,"[24] but there are other necessities as well which science does not satisfy, our "affective and volitive necessities."[24]

As it appears, then, Unamuno considers science as an elaborate recipe, constantly refined according to definite rules and because of definite needs, a recipe in which the ingredients are named and the steps carefully listed, but which gives neither the ingredients themselves nor the desire to cook. Its universality is that of empty forms, and without men of flesh and bones who give it life by making it subjectively true to themselves it would rather appear as an empty wasps' nest: geometrical and bare. Moreover, without the men of flesh and bones who have elaborated it, wanting it to be, and, willing it, created it, it would not even be at the disposal of our whim and need. "It is not the intelligence, but rather the will, that makes the world for us, and the old Scholastic aphorism: *nihil volitum quin praecognitum*, nothing is wanted which before has not been known, must be corrected with a: *nihil cognitum quin praevolitum*, nothing is known which before has not been wanted."[25] The science of the head points to the wisdom of the heart.

Finally, lest these forms be interpreted as some sort of incorporeal *lekta* similar to what the Old Stoics are held to have meant,[26] Unamuno maintains that they themselves have an "inside as we ourselves do, and just as we not only know ourselves, but *are* also *being ourselves,* they *are.*"[27] Indeed, "everything has entrails, everything has an inside, including science,"[27] and "if inside the forms there is quantity, inside of this there is quality, the intraquantitative, the *quid divinum.*"[27] To know, to intuit this "being" is the work of love,[27] and love is the wisdom of the heart. Consequently, whereas the emphasis upon the objective part of the criterion of truth leads to the purely intellectual elaboration

22

of an "apparent" world severed from that of concrete experience, the emphasis upon the subjective part of the criterion leads to the "intimate penetration of the substantial world,"[28] the truth of which is "personal and incommunicable."[29] "Reason unites us, and the truth separates us."[29]

Against the science of the head, reason, and the intelligence, Unamuno finds the wisdom of the heart, sentience, the imagination, the will;[30] against logic and its identities, love and uniqueness ("When I hear the groan of my neighbor, who, to the eye is a form fitting other forms, I feel sorrow in my entrails and through love, the revelation of *being*").[31] These antithetical lists should not be taken, however, as indicative of some general classification in the Kantian manner. The only point Unamuno wishes to stress, is the unbridgeable cleavage between the objective and the subjective realms. Reason cannot "open itself to the revelation of life."[32] Subjective knowledge is not susceptible of being formalized: its symbolization is hazardous and leads to misunderstanding.

There are, for Unamuno, terms which are amenable to logical definition and others which are not. The latter belong solely to the subjective realm, and any attempt to force them into the objective one is doomed to failure. One of these terms is the word "God," "because God is undefinable."[33] "My idea of God is different each time that I conceive it."[34] Another such term is the name of a man for " 'not even I myself seize all that I am' "[35]; a true man can only be subjectively known because he "reveals himself, creates himself, in a moment, in a sentence, in a shout,"[36] and the act or the shout remains a unique experience that cannot be equated to any other thing. Each one of us is the development of his own symbol,[37] therefore, that symbol can never be equated to any other set of symbols.

Contrariwise, there are terms which may be defined in the objective realm, but which cannot be experienced and therefore lack all meaning in the subjective one. Death is one such term: it can be defined, its use can be regulated, it can only be experienced once: "We cannot conceive of ourselves as non-existent."[38]

Thus the very tools of each realm are different, and it is an illusion, according to Unamuno, to think that all terms are equally amenable to subjective and objective handling.

The subjective is properly the realm of the here and now. Its criterion bears upon what is being believed in this time and in this place by the person who professes here and now a certain belief. At the root of this belief is an affective state which motivates the striving towards the realization of a particular idea or another: "to believe is in the first instance to want to believe,"[39] "to believe is to create."[40] Unamuno calls "will" the faculty which drives man to know,[41] and "imagination" the faculty which enables man to create.[42] Those are not, however, hard and fast definitions to which Unamuno has felt bound in whatever he wrote; on the contrary. When he used these terms, he used them in this way most of the time. Often, however, he gave their task to love, to a vital desire, to anguish. Possibly the right interpretation is that they are expressions of a vital force distinguished in their functions but not in their nature, which is that vital force itself.

The "method of the heart," Unamuno calls *cardiaca*[43] because "it is dangerous to call logic"[43] such a method. He sometimes names it also *biotica*.[44] This "method" is love, as it appears from such texts as this: "When I hear the groan of my neighbor, who to the eye is a form fitting other forms, I feel sorrow in my entrails and through love, the revelation of *being*. Through love we get to things with our own *being*, not with the mind alone, we make them *fellow beings*."[45]

"Sexual love is the generating type of another love";[46] there are in Unamuno's conception two different levels of love, distinguishable in form, if not in aim. The first level is that of merely carnal love, which is "the love between man and woman to perpetuate the human race on Earth."[47] The second level, that of "spiritual love,"[48] born of desperation, "Because men only love each other with spiritual love when they have suffered together a same sorrow,"[48] is properly compassion,[49] that is to say, to suffer within one's own self the pain the person loved is seen to suffer. It is this love which is the "method" of the heart, and as such it possesses different facets depending upon the object of its compassion.

Love, of either level, is the "instinct of perpetuation,"[50] but whereas, "what lovers perpetuate on the Earth is the flesh of sorrow, is sorrow, is death,"[51] compassion strives to perpetuate consciousness.[52] The compassionate man, because he is compassionate, assimilates to himself all that towards which he feels compassion. That is to say, he personalizes everything.

> Love personalizes all it loves. One only falls in love with an idea personalizing it. And when love is so great and so vivid, and so strong and overflowing that everything is loved, then everything is personalized and it is discovered that the total All, that the Universe, is a Person also who has Consciousness, Consciousness which in its turn suffers, sympathizes and loves; that is to say, is consciousness.

And to this Consciousness of the Universe that love discovers personalizing all it loves, we give the name God.[53]

This compassion and this personalization should not be construed, however, as liable to be acquired once and for all, or to be felt once and for all. It is the distinctive property of subjective truth as Unamuno sees it, that it must be felt here and now, lived here and now. Thus "as soon as love sees its vital desire realized, it becomes sad and discovers immediately that this toward which it tended is not its proper aim,"[54] and proceeds on to search anew. A subjective truth is all the more true that it is less susceptible of corroboration, subjective or objective. "Love looks and tends always toward the future, since its work is the work of our perpetuation; the property of love is to hope, and it maintains itself only with hope."[54]

The compassionate man must, therefore, be continuously compassionate, and that means that he must personalize everything he can. In order to do so, he must not only feel his own anguish, but that of every other thing. "The universal sorrow is the anguish of everything to be everything else without being able to achieve it, to be each what it is, being at the same time everything which it is not, and being it forever."[55] And this universal sorrow is at the root of the universal love mentioned earlier. The two notions of sorrow and love are, in Unamuno's conception, complementary.

Subjective knowledge, therefore, through compassion and sorrow, reveals the unique being of that which it knows, this revelation is assimilation, and an assimilation that works both ways: the knowing being, man, personalizes the thing known, and in order to do so has to put himself in the place of the thing, so to speak. "To know anything is to make myself be that which I know."[56] Whereas the intelligence dissolves the object, whereas it needs only ideas in order to operate, love (in the text to which I refer Unamuno uses "the will," but under his pen this term seems to denote a facet of love) needs matter,[56] love needs something to love.

Although the term "love" itself cannot be objectively defined, but must be felt in order to be known,[57] the object of love may be in some way symbolized, expressed in all its momentaneous presence by the work of art. "In art, in fact, we search for an imitation of eternalization. If in the beautiful the soul calms itself and rests and recovers, though the anguish is not cured, it is because the beautiful is the revelation of the eternal, of the divine of things, and beauty is nothing other than the

25

perpetuation of momentariness."[58] Such creation is the work of the imagination, "the faculty for creating images,"[59] be they verbal or otherwise. Even science makes use of the product of the imagination, the metaphor, and language.[60] Science also, therefore, can be a work of love, when it is a work of creation, when it is directed toward the fact, "but the total and live fact, the marvellous fact of universal life, rooted in mysteries,"[61] for "the whole Universe is a texture of facts in the sea of the indistinct and the indetermined."[62] And Unamuno once again modifies the *nihil volitum quin praecognitum* to read *nihil cognitum quin praevolitum,* but making precise that "nothing can be well known which is not loved, which is not sympathized with."[63]

Thus subjective knowledge and objective knowledge fuse in the act of knowing, even objectively, though in all other respects they are hopelessly at odds, subjective knowledge being never completely transmitted by any symbolization. And just as reason and intelligence reached a universality by lifting their knowledge into a system independent of any specific time and place, subjective knowledge reaches also a universality, but it is the universality of the unique, experienced once and for all time. "The absolutely individual is the absolutely universal, since even in logic the individual propositions are identified with the universal ones."[64] "That which is of each man, is of all men."[64] And that which is subjectively true to any one man is therefore subjectively true once and for all and for all men, for "each one of us is unique and irreplaceable,"[65] "each one of us is absolute."[65] That is to say, each one of us, with all his lived experience partakes of the concrete or subjective definition of the word man, contributing his own individual experience to the whole picture, much as the distinctive applications of paint in an Impressionist work contribute to the whole picture while retaining their individuality and uniqueness.

Just as the scientist, that is to say, the sage, feels love for this earth he understands, so does the artist who feels it,[66] and of these, the poet, "he who gives us a whole world personalized, a complete world made man, the word made world,"[67] is, in Unamuno's estimation, the closest to the mystics who searched "in the depth of the soul, in its central and intimate being, in the interior castle, the 'substance of the secrets,' the living law of the Universe,"[68] the culmination of subjective knowledge.

Though they fuse in one point, subjective and objective knowledge are hopelessly at odds. The task "to conciliate the intellectual necessities with the affective necessities and the volitive ones"[69] Unamuno places upon philosophy. "Philosophy answers the necessity to form for ourselves a unitary and total conception of the world and of life,"[70] it "refers itself to our whole destiny, to our action towards life and the Universe."[71] It must, therefore, take into account the vital desire which drives us on, the continuous striving as well as the goal towards which it prods us, and it must, as well, take into account the knowledge that science has put at our disposal to tell us whether or not that goal "fails in the theoretical or practical reality,"[72] or whether this theoretical reality has nothing to do with it at all. Philosophy, therefore, inasmuch as it must be attentive to both the heart and the head, inasmuch as it must be "our manner of understanding or of not understanding the world and life,"[73] must as well be subjectively true. "We must say, above all, that philosophy is more related to poetry than to science,"[73] in that it is not a description of what is, nor yet a description of what has been, but an attempt to describe, to symbolize, that which one strives to create. It is the reflection of the ideal that one has of one's self.[74]

Such a philosophy must be an attempt to symbolize what is in fact lived by the person, it "stems from our feeling towards life itself."[75] It is present in the language, "And to such a point is it thus, that it is fitting to maintain that there are as many philosophies as idioms and as many variants of these as dialects, including what we might call the individual dialect."[76] It is a concrete philosophy.[77]

To express such a philosophy in an adequate way, with life, with as much concreteness as possible, presuming that the words are understood concretely in the same way by all and writing accordingly, is not enough. Such a philosophy must be lived by the reader as much as it has been by the writer if it is to be done justice. It must be a presentation of the individual truth of the writer, universal because it is individual. It must, in fact, bend language to its use and force the reader to pay attention and live as much as he may—render subjectively true to himself—what he reads. It is this problem of concrete expression which is at the root of Unamuno's choice of form, of means of expression. And this choice he clearly stated in the very first pages of his first book-length publication:

> First of all, it is proper for me to inform the reader with a bureau-
> cratic and syllogistic mind that here nothing is proved with certifi-
> cates either historical or of any other type, such as he would mean by
> proof; that this is not a work that he would call *science;* that here
> there will be only rhetoric to him who ignores that the syllogism is a
> mere figure of diction. It behooves me also to forewarn each reader
> with respect to the dry and cutting affirmations that he will read here,

27

and to the *contradictions* which he will expect to find. It is accustomed to search for the complete truth in the *golden mean* by the method of removal, *via remocionis,* by exclusion of the extremes, which with their play and mutual action engender the rhythm of life, and thus one reaches only a shadow of truth, cold and nebulous. It is preferable, I believe, to follow another method: that of the alternative affirmation of the contradictories; it is preferable to make the force of the extremes gush in the soul of the reader, so that the mean take in it life, which is the result of struggle.[78]

By affirming alternately what science shows to be objectively true, and what the heart shows to be subjectively true on any one subject, the whole problem, as it presents itself to Unamuno, is exposed, and, in a sense, the solution also. Where objective truth has the definite last word, as in some mathematical question or another, Unamuno would be the last to dispute the answer, and indeed would only insist that those who accept it as true had lived it enough to know the reason why it is mathematically true. But on all subjects in which reason cannot have the last word, then the affirmation of both positions is necessary. Because these will stem from different parts of the criterion of truth they will necessarily be opposed. From this opposition will stem doubt and from doubt the necessity to invent, that is to say, to create a solution of one's own.

The problem of philosophy is this: "What is the goal of the whole universe? Such is the enigma of the Sphinx; he who, in one way or another, does not solve it, is devoured."[79] Toward its solution Unamuno marshals all the findings of science, all the aspirations of the mystics and the poets, all his own beliefs. All his works are a continuous attempt at a solution. In them alternate affirmations constituting what he sometimes calls "the apparent order of things"[80] with what he considers to be "substantial revelations."[81] Together, they constitute the Unamunian Weltanschauung, voluntarily cryptic, challenging, elusive, within which lies the concrete lesson he wanted to impart.

Knowledge is something live, something which must be alive in the knower if it is really known. To impart knowledge is not to state answers, but to state problems, though it is, perhaps, to state them in such a way that what is presumed to be the right answer should be within sight. The challenge Unamuno accepted and fought was the one of the dead letter, of the lifeless text. He made his the exhortation he wrote to Spanish universities, attempting that each one of his books and each one of his actions be a "workshop, and not a bazaar of ideas."[82]

4. "QUIXOTIC" EXISTENTIALISM
Part 1: Weltanschauung

The emphasis which the Unamunian theory of knowledge and criterion of truth place upon actual experience makes of the individual human being the focal point of philosophy; that is to say, the life of the individual human being then becomes the record of his actual beliefs, the text of his actual philosophy. When Unamuno affirms that "this concrete man, of flesh and bone, is the subject and the supreme object, at the same time, of all philosophy,"[1] he affirms nothing but a direct consequence of his criterion of truth, namely, that philosophy cannot be an abstract intellectual game only, it must be subjectively true, it must be experienced, it must be the expression of the man's experience of the world and of life. "Our philosophy . . . stems from our feeling with respect to life itself, and this, like all the affective, has subconscious, even perhaps inconscious roots."[2]

The universality of the unique which Unamuno asserts,[3] and the uniqueness of the absolute ("everything is absolute, absolute in itself, relative in relation to the others"),[4] together with his theory of abstraction as a process analogous to the obtention of common features by compound photography,[5] buttress his claim that philosophy needs be both the product of a private "sentience,"[6] or be it even "presentiment,"[6] and "the total vision of the Universe and of life through an ethnical temperament,"[7] referring itself to "our whole destiny, our attitude in front of life and the Universe."[8] Each man, therefore, willy nilly, lives a philosophy of his own which he inscribes in his actions and in his language, consciously or otherwise, and in so doing he contributes to the overall picture of man; ὁ ἄνθρωπος is defined by τοῖς πολλοῖς ἀνδράσι, that is to say, by the compound image obtained in superimposing each individual ἄνδρα —his life and his acts—one upon the other. The primacy of individual belief, of private sentiment, over common consent corresponds to the primacy of experience over expression: "It is not customary that our ideas be that which makes us optimists, but rather that our optimism or our pessimism, of a physiological or perhaps even pathological order, the one just as much as the other, be that which makes our ideas."[9] Philosophy, therefore, will be, indeed must be, closer to poetry than to science,[9] it is the expression each man gives to his experience of life as he lives it.

29

The philosophy a man expresses, i.e., writes down, can no longer be construed as programmatic or prescriptive, as would be, for example, a set of moral laws, it can only be considered as descriptive, an approximation of what seems to be to the author his experience of life and the universe at the time of the actual writing. A later approximation may contain some entirely different claims, if the man's experience of life has for some reason radically changed. The first and only binding allegiance of any man is to his own experience, such and as it appears to him to be. And Unamuno loudly vindicates "the inalienable right to contradict myself, to be each day new, without letting, for all that, to be always the same, to affirm my distinct aspects while working so that my life integrate them."[10] For "every philosophic theory serves to explain and justify an ethic, a doctrine of conduct, which surges in reality from the intimate moral sentiment of its own author. . . . Our doctrines, customarily, are nothing but the a posteriori justification of our conduct, or the manner in which we try to explain it ourselves to our own self."[11]

This primacy of the inner private daemon, this world-weary realization that reasons are mostly rationalizations, Unamuno mercilessly proves in his critique of some of the most scrupulous defenders of right reason, such as Kant, for example, pointing out, after Kierkegaard, the "jump" between the *Critique of Pure Reason* and the *Critique of Practical Reason*.[12] "Philosophy is the human product of each philosopher, and each philosopher is a man of flesh and bone who addresses himself to other men of flesh and bone like himself. And, whatever he may wish, he philosophizes, not with reason only, but rather with the will, with the sentience, with the flesh and with the bones, with the whole soul and the whole body. The man philosophizes."[13] And a man who attempts to be a philosopher in spite of his humanity, that is to say who abstracts his thought from his sentience, " 'such an abstract thinker is a double being, a fantastic being who lives in the pure being of abstraction, and at the same time the sad figure of a professor who sets aside this abstract essence as he does a walking-stick' ";[14] "he is, above all, a pedant, that is to say, a mockery of man."[15]

Thus philosophy is the deed of the individual. It is a rationalization. "One more time I must repeat that our ethical and philosophical doctrines, in general, are usually nothing but the a posteriori justification of our conduct, of our actions. Our doctrines are usually the means we seek to explain and justify to others and to our own self, our own modus operandi."[16] Translated in terms of Unamuno's theory of language, philosophy is the expression given by a man to the experience of life as

30

he lives it, the attempt to fix with words and thus crystallize in an individual and distinctive mark his unique presence. And when Unamuno in the same paragraph writes that "the sentiment, not the rational conception of the universe and of life, reflects itself better than in a philosophical system or than in a realist novel, in a poem" and that "I count among the great novels—or epic poems, it is all the same—with the *Iliad* and the *Odyssey* and the *Divine Comedy* and the Quixote and *Paradise Lost* and the *Faust,* also the *Ethics* of Spinoza, and the *Critique of Pure Reason* of Kant, and the Logic of Hegel,"[17] one should not see there a contradiction and yell: "Nonsense!" but rather understand that in each of these works an absolute experience of a unique human destiny is partially salvaged, in the same manner as a metaphor, a paradox, a verse, singly preserve a unique moment, feeling, thought or fancy.

The truth of a philosophic doctrine, even the most coherent, can only be, therefore, that given to it by the life of the man who elaborated it and his sincerity in doing so. None, in their frozen formulation can again be true to anyone, because to experience the text in which they are preserved is to live it, and to live it is a totally new experience which itself needs be expressed in its own terms. When Francisco Zababilde, Pachico, Unamuno's alter ego in his novel *Paz en la Guerra,* says that "the dogmas had been true at one time, true while they were produced, but now they are neither true nor false, having lost all substance and all sense,"[18] he may be made by Unamuno to exaggerate the point a little, but he nevertheless affirms a fundamental tenet of Unamunian thought, the preface, as it were, and a special caution to be taken with respect to his philosophy. His thought is not to be considered as the long awaited answer to all philosophical problems, it is not offered as such, it is only the thought of the man Unamuno, from which it is hoped that, by comparison with other works, some main lines may be discerned by subsequent thinkers with respect to the problems of man as they will appear to them then. Each philosopher presents a little facet of the truth,[19] all contribute to it, yet, "Every philosophical sentence, thus, every axiom, every general and solemn proposition, aphoristically enunciated, is a stupidity,"[20] because unless it is part of a unitary living experience it can pretend only to satisfy part of the criterion of truth, the lesser part, the common one.

Philosophy, therefore, remains fettered to the private total experience of the human being who lives a particular thought. It is an attempt by that human being to explain to himself and to others his actions, his

31

presence, his own intimate "motive of life" as he himself would like to think it to be. Thus at the base of any philosophy is the lone, frightened, puny man looking at that which he thinks to be his past, that which he thinks to be his present, that which he thinks to be his future, and wondering painfully as he feels his body growing old, his time of life escaping from this body (for "πάντα ὥσπερ κεράμια ῥεῖ"),[21] and asking "why?" in order to know "what for" or whither."[22]

This primordial "moment" in the life of the individual, when, for the first time, he feels himself be through the anguish of becoming incessantly, this birth of self-consciousness as it may be called, may happen any time, but it always is a confrontation with one's total destiny, a putting in question of one's total destiny, in short, the intimate, emotional consciousness of the possibility of one's own death,[23] the awareness of "the tragic feeling of life,"[24] as Unamuno himself called it.

It is also the recognition of one's uniqueness, of one's total irreplaceability: "Each one is unique and cannot be substituted;"[25] "I am something entirely new;"[26] "there is no other I."[26] And this recognition is simultaneous with both the fear of death and the desire to remain alive, "the longing to live"[27] that drives each living thing on, be it called "instinct of conservation,"[28] or "instinct of perpetuation,"[28] "hunger,"[28] or "love,"[28] or all those names at the same time.

This fundamental moment, which one might call with François Meyer the "Unamunian *cogito*,"[29] does not occur *in vacuo*. It happens to a man who has already lived a number of years, any Alonso Quijano in any country, whose thought has been conditioned by all the *idola fori* of his own language and of his private experience, but who, under the fist of pain, or sorrow, looks upon himself and feels himself to be in a sort of spiritual "synaesthesis."[30] The event is not dissimilar to the painful revelation of the presence of a tooth to its owner when the slow erosion of decay finally reaches a critical spot. It is at this point that the philosophical investigation begins.[31]

The Unamunian *cogito*, therefore, consists in the adventitious revelation of one's own existence through the pain inflicted on one's own self by the uncertainty of one's future prospects. In this, the role of reason is quite preponderant, not, as for Descartes, as the guide and the prompter, but rather as the necessary tool, in a negative manner:

> Reason, the human reason, within its limits, not only does not prove rationally that the soul be immortal and that the human consciousness has to be in the series of the forthcoming times, but proves rather, within its limits, I repeat, that the individual consciousness

cannot persist after the death of the corporeal organism on which it depends. And these limits within which I say that the human reason proves this, are the limits of rationality, of what we know by proof.[32]

Reason, therefore, exacerbates the "longing to live" by confronting it with the rational, or reasonable, possibility of its own cessation, a possibility that is not subjectively true, because "we cannot conceive ourselves as nonexisting,"[33] that is to say, we can experience this only once and therefore before we do, it is never more than abstractly mentioned. To attempt to picture to oneself what that possibility might mean in terms of one of our own experiences, albeit the last one, "causes a most anguishing vertigo."[33] The power of this "longing" becomes all the more apparent as the prospects of its being continuously satisfied grow darker.

With the help of reason, however, and under the guise of its sanction, attempts may be made, and have been made to substitute for the certainty of one's own immortality, the certainty of one's own appurtenance to an overall, presumably immortal, state of things. But "abstract thought does not serve my immortality except to kill me as an individual singularly existing, and thus to make me immortal, more or less in the manner of that doctor from Holberg, who with his medicine removed the life of the patient, but removed also the fever!"[34] Reason, social product based upon abstractions of language and the method of logic, cannot deal with the exclusively individual and therefore cannot account for even the mere presence on earth of one single specific individual, let alone for his own specific survival: it can only deal with abstract entities and not with any one man.

Furthermore, in all rigor, "with respect to the concrete vital problem in which we are interested, reason does not take any position."[35] It cannot. For Unamuno, the "concrete vital problem" is his innermost individual experience: in its uniqueness it cannot fall under the sway of reason. The general case, the paradigm, let us say, cannot be used because the important thing is not the compromise which answers statistically, but the one solution which is but an item in the statistical picture. Thus even if reason would allow the absolute negation of the immortality of the soul in general, which, in Unamuno's view, it doesn't,[36] its answer could not be applied to the new special case except as a probability; that is to say, in effect, that it would not apply at all in the concrete way. It is through this tiny keyhole of uncertainty that Unamuno squeezes an attempt at a solution.

If reason could provide a solution by either proving the individual's

33

immortality or total mortality with the same degree of certainty as it does that "the three angles of a triangle are equal to two right angles . . . either certainty would make life impossible to us."[37] The moment of "synaesthesis" which, under the prodding of a feeling of anguish toward our whole future, opened the way to the questioning and would then result in either certainty, would itself be a perfectly gratuitous thing, and the consciousness of which it is the awakening would also be perfectly gratuitous. But for Unamuno, "If consciousness is nothing more, as said some inhumane thinker, than a flash between two eternities of darkness, then there is nothing more execrable than existence."[38] Because, if one dies completely, then nothing has meaning;[39] because if death is an eternal sleep "without dreams nor awakening,"[40] then the longing for immortality is madness,[40] then, "are right in this world only the Bachellors Carrascos, the Dukes, the Don Antonio Morenos, who, as jesters, finally, make of courage and goodness a pastime and joy of their idleness."[40] And the certainty of immortality leads to no better prospect for:

> The strongest basis for uncertainty, what makes our vital desire waver the most, what gives the most efficiency to the dissolving work of reason, is to make ourselves consider what a life of the soul after death could be. Because, even vanquishing, through a powerful effort of faith, reason which tells us and teaches that the soul is nothing but a function of the organized body, there remains for us the need to imagine what an immortal and eternal life of the soul could be. In this imagination the contradictions and the absurdities multiply themselves, and one reaches, perhaps, the conclusion of Kierkegaard, which is that, if the mortality of the soul is terrible, not the less terrible is its immortality.[41]

Beatific visions appear "either as annihilation proper or as a prolonged boredom,"[42] or even as "a return to unconsciousness through lack of shock, of difference, or be it of activity."[43] Thus, all of these considerations liberally provided deny the desire for life and in so doing augment the evidence of its presence and that of its strength.

At this stage of the Unamunian *cogito*, all that the individual human being possesses is the consciousness of his own existence through the consciousness of pain in the form of anguish, or in the form of longing, desire, want, dire want of more life. This longing cannot be objectively satisfied, but it remains subjectively true for as long as it is felt. Reason, therefore, by exacerbating it, all the while contributed to its existence itself, and the feeling, through its constant tug at the sentience, keeps consciousness turned upon its owner, who can only repeat with Una-muno: "In one word: with the reason, without the reason or against it, I have no intention to see myself die" (*no me da la gana de morirme*).⁴⁴ It is at the price of this suffering that consciousness remains subjectively true: it must be continuously experienced, and it can only be con-tinuously experienced through pain, longing or sorrow.⁴⁵ "And how can one know that he exists without suffering a little or much? How can one turn toward himself, acquire reflexive consciousness, if it be not through sorrow? When one rejoices, one lets himself forget about himself, that he exists; one passes to another, to the alien, alienates himself. And one turns himself to his own self, returns upon his own self, to being his own self, only in sorrow."⁴⁶ The peculiar sorrow that is the want of love, the longing of love, leads one to consciousness, and consciousness is the only thing truly real, because "the only thing truly real is that which feels, suffers, compassionates, loves and longs, it is consciousness; the only thing that is substantial is consciousness."⁴⁷

This affirmation of the self inherent in the Unamunian *cogito* is un-intelligible to reason. Unamuno, who, when dealing with matters of objective knowledge, takes his information from the most extreme positivists, considers as the case in point the thesis of the behaviorists with respect to consciousness, according to which, "consciousness is the inaccessible mystery, or the unknowable."⁴⁸ Science, for Unamuno, "destroys the concept of personality, reducing it to a complexity in continuous momentaneous flux; that is to say, it destroys the sentimental basis of the life of the spirit, which, without surrendering, turns itself against reason."⁴⁹ In other words, the unique individual certainty of one's own existence finds no support in science or in reason, since both conspire to describe it as an adventitious consequence of sundry forces which do not account for its uniqueness at all, on the contrary. It is at this crucial point that the choice must be made between the two parts of the criterion of truth and a decision reached as to which one is primor-dial to the other: "in the starting point" are those "who put men above ideas and those who put ideas above men."⁵⁰ "Everything reduces to the estimation of a preference between two values, and in every ques-tion of this kind it is more the decision of the sentience than of the reason."⁵⁰

For Unamuno, any decision being made by anyone in this respect is a matter of sentience, of rationalization, not of logical necessity, and therefore, it is the man who in fact takes precedence no matter what his own ultimate choice may be. Thus he affirms as above and beyond the

35

reach of reason the sentimental certainty of his own consciousness, and, as evidence of this certainty, all that he has is the present experience of it through pain. Where the objective part of the criterion of truth is of no help, all that remains is the subjective part with its stipulations and limitations in time and place. The certainty of the existence of one's own consciousness is bound to the present experience of it. When that experience ceases, self-consciousness ceases also, and one goes back to sleep "in the small boat of habit letting (oneself) be carried along by the waters."[51]

The Unamunian *cogito*, therefore, is the reverse of the Cartesian one, as Unamuno himself points out: "The truth is *sum, ergo cogito* ('I am, therefore I think,') even though not all that which is thinks."[52] And, for Unamuno, the life of the being which merely is, is not a true life,[52] for to experience one's own self as being is the only way to make this being subjectively true to one's own self. Any other attempt to ascertain this being, as for example Descartes', gives an abstract knowledge of it, not the concrete experience which alone is self-warranting.[52] Any other attempt requires the corroboration of reason, and that corroboration is just what reason cannot give.

This consciousness of the vital desire which is the self is, therefore, "not properly a problem, it cannot take a logical form, it cannot formulate itself in propositions rationally discussable, but it plants itself in us as hunger plants itself in us."[53] And it is when it plants itself thus, when it is at work in us, that it exists in a concrete way. To all those who place the man above his reason, therefore, "only that which works exists and to exist is to work:"[54] in the present case of self-consciousness, such a consciousness exists only while it works upon the man, forcing him to "turn upon himself," upon his destiny, and to read the events of his own life as he would a book, proposing to him "the terrible problem of whether to finish reading the novel that has converted itself into his life, and to die finishing it, or to renounce reading it and to live, to live, and consequently to die also."[55]

But that prospect of death is only a possibility, it is only a theoretical possibility, and though it is at the heart of the problem which confronts consciousness it is not the only one. Or rather, it is only a form under which the problem of consciousness presents itself. The innate texture of that problem is pain, "and the only mystery truly mysterious is the mystery of pain."[56] Pain is that which brings consciousness to being, it is that completely irrational unitary element at the root of the individual, that unique, incommunicable private resonance which can be labeled, analyzed into sets of causes, but never reduplicated: it is the perfectly unique and irretrievable.

The form of that problem, that to which the cause of the pain is ascribed and of which death is but an aspect, is "the sensation of one's own limit."[56] "The consciousness of one's own self is nothing other than the consciousness of one's own limitation."[56] This limitation is a limitation in time, in place,[57] in thought,[58] in matter.[58] To exist "really and truly" in time and place, one has to feel time and place, to experience them, the former as a continuous loss, the latter as a continuous lack: one has to suffer not to be eternal and infinite,[57] otherwise time and place are not really experienced, are not really needed, longed for, known through desire and love, as anything that is to be known subjectively must be known. Likewise, "thought is limited by the word"[58] which never is adequate, never is the lived living experience, and therefore always maims what it only partially salvages. And finally, the pain felt and experienced by the consciousness through consciousness is "the obstacle that matter puts to the mind; it is the shock of consciousness with the unconscious;"[58] it is the experience of one's own body, of one's own matter, of one's being in the apparent or rational order of things.

Consciousness, then, is pain and sorrow, and as reason leaves it unexplained, unable to warrant it in any way, "If you look at the Universe the closest and the deepest that you can look at it, which is within your own self, if you feel and not just contemplate things all in your consciousness, where all of them have left their painful trace, you will reach the depth of tedium, not just the tedium of life but of something more: the tedium of existence, the well of the vanity of vanities."[59] Within oneself there is nothing more than that which reason sees, nothing but a complex of forces in continuous flux, adventitious and superfluous, nothing that is, except the feeling of pain which, upon becoming conscious of this nothingness, one feels. "You yourself seek your own self! But when you meet yourself, is it not that you meet with nothingness proper?"[60] "And it is thus that you will get to compassionate everything, to the universal love."[59]

For love and pain, for Unamuno, seem to be the two faces of a same coin. To love is to want, and to want in such dire need that the wanting is a pain. Thus the "mystery of love" is that of pain,[61] the two are indissolubly united. And their "form," which is the form of the consciousness of which they are the stuff, is time:[61] "We tie yesterday to tomorrow with links of anguish, and now is, strictly speaking, nothing other than the effort of before trying to become after; the present is

37

nothing but the insistence of the past to make itself future. Now is a point which, not well defined, dissipates itself, and, nevertheless, in this point lies the whole eternity, the substance of time."[61]

In the moment of self-consciousness, the moment of the awareness of personal striving through the pain it causes, lies all of time. Time, for Unamuno, is not the discrete succession of events, it is a continuous present of striving, not the abstract mention of the morrow, not the mechanical carving of clocks. "The true future is today."[62] The concrete experience of time is the present longing for something to come, the present demand for more time, the actual expectation in fear and anguish of another morrow, and beyond that one, still another, ad infinitum. Thus it is that the present remains in fact unchanging, that "eternity is the substance of time, as the sea is the substance of the waves."[63] Since the moment of self-consciousness finds no help in reason or language but must, in order to be at all, be continuously experienced, it cannot be said to have been, or to recur, or to be experienced anew, for to say that is merely to use empty abstract phrases with little evidence of their truth: the maimed memory, in words, of an experience to which reason gives no support. All that it possesses as evidence of itself, is therefore its own self, and that solely to the individual feeling it, while he feels it. All that reason considers as time must therefore be included in that peculiar moment, it being then an eternal present, the unmoving eye of one's own consciousness watching one's own life go by: "Your life is before your own consciousness the continuous revelation, in time, of your eternity, the development of your symbol, you go on discovering your self as you work."[64] The Unamunian *cogito* is the revelation to one's own self of its own presence as unmoved spectator, a tiny mirror reflecting the whole magnificent show and striving in all its particles to go on reflecting it, and in that one instant, unchanging, being eternally. Just as Homer framed the seizure of Troy, the war and all attendant circumstances within the wrath of Achilles, so, Unamuno affirms, is the whole universe framed within the unchanging instantaneity of one lone human self-consciousness. There can be no experience more fundamental than that self-consciousness, and though there can be experiences of which we are conscious without being conscious of that consciousness, these experiences are not as fundamental as the other: "To be is not the same thing as to be one's self. An animal, be it human, is; a person is his self."[65] Unamuno uses here a reflexive form of the Spanish verb *ser*, *serse*, a verb which, by contradistinction with the other Spanish verb to be, *estar*, denotes absolute, irrevocable being, unique in time and forever equal unto itself, as, for example, facts of birth and death.

At the root of self-consciousness, therefore, is memory,[66] "the basis of individual personality;"[66] memory is that conglomeration of memories upon which consciousness turns when it becomes self-consciousness: "One lives in the remembrance and for the remembrance, and our spiritual life is nothing else than, at bottom, the effort of our remembrance to persevere, to make itself hope, the effort of our past to make itself future."[66] This effort is self-love:

> According as you enter within your own self and in your self your self deepen, you go on discovering your own inanity, for you are not all that you were, for you are not that which you would be, for you are, finally, nothing more than a mere nothing. And when you touch your own inanity, when you do not feel your own permanent fund, when you do not reach either your own infinity or even less your own eternity, you pity yourself with all your heart, and you kindle yourself with a painful love for your own self, killing what is called self-love and is nothing but a sort of sensual delectation of yourself, something like the self-enjoyment of the flesh of your soul.
>
> The spiritual love for one's self, the compassion that one acquires for one's own self, may perhaps be called egotism, but it is the most opposed to vulgar egoism.[67]

It is through this love and compassion that the revelation of being is made: the self-consciousness in all its differing aspects which Unamuno has taken great pleasure and great pains to disperse and entangle leads therefore to this lone revelation. All that is real so far is the feeling of love and pain, all the rest, the memories, the spectacle, the scenes that pass in front of us "as in a cinema," have so far no intrinsic existence except as we are conscious of being conscious of them: "There is an exterior environment, the world of sensible phenomena which surrounds and supports us, and an interior environment, our own consciousness, the world of our ideas, imaginations, desires, and feelings. No one can say where one ends and the other begins; no one can trace the dividing line, no one can say up to what point we are of the exterior world or it is ours."[68] As a matter of fact, to those who do not have the fundamental experience of self-consciousness, the question does not arise: "in life one does not discuss metaphysically, and when people start to eat, they never think whether the foods they take have an objective reality or not."[69] It is only when the individual casts a worried look upon his fleeting existence and in the anguished apprehension of the possibility of his own annihilation grasps at all the possible reassurances that the question of the objective reality of it all poses itself. Otherwise, life is just a fleeting spectacle, a dream, as for example, it is assumed to be for the people of Brianzuelo in the following text:

—This hamlet, Brianzuelo, is beautiful! It has nothing to see and much to feel! Do you not feel it, do you not feel it in your veins already? Do you not hear its silence? Look, look at this cow. . . . Did it ever occur to it to look sometimes at the clouds and to think about what they may be?

—Oh no! The spirit of the cows has nothing nebulous or of the dreamer . . . I suppose. It is like the spirit of the peasants, who never dream.

—Who never dream? I believe that they do nothing else. Or do you believe that while they work they think, what we ourselves call thinking? No, no: they dream, they do nothing more than dream. . . .

—And what do they dream?

—What? What they have in front of their eyes: the concrete and present reality, the field, the ox that passes by, the bird that flies. . . .

—Is it that they see it?

—No; it is that they dream it. Their soul is what they have in front of them: the universe, an immense cloud that changes ceaselessly . . . until it dissolves itself for them into rain.

—And it rains?

—Yes; it rains upon their tomb; it rains time in ceaseless drops.[70]

"Life is a dream," then, in the immortal words of Calderón,[71] or: "We are such stuff / As dreams are made on,"[71] as Shakespeare would have it, "and in these we have substantial revelations,"[71] and consciousness is, therefore, that revelation, the only certainty, the only affirmation of which one can be absolutely sure, and the problem remains completely, namely, "What is the end of the whole universe?"[72] and principally, what is the purpose of that consciousness to which the destiny of the whole seems bound?

For it is now obvious that the only consciousness ever absolutely substantial to one's own self is one's own, and that therefore there is no difference between the problem of one's own individual immortality and that "of all those whom I have dreamt and am dreaming . . . that of all those who dream me and whom I dream. Immortality, like the dream, is either communal or it is not."[73] Understand, either the dream is a matter of objective knowledge in which everyone partakes and thus it becomes completely true, or it is the private certainty of one individual and thus ceases to be true whenever that individual ceases to give it subjective truth. The anguished consciousness feeling itself be, watching itself being, is anguished because all it possesses is that present certainty through a present feeling which may cease, and which, by ceasing, returns the consciousness back into nothingness. The problem of "immortality" viewed under this light, is primarily that of the continuation of a single present moment, of a single present relationship of the conscious being to himself, namely his own aspiration to be, his own yearning to continue being, his desire to continue to watch the dream go by, knowing all the while that the "pain" he feels is his own presence, the one anchor which enables him to single himself out from the spectacle and be himself, and thus being to give that much of a subjective existence to the rest of the dream.

The fact that reason is of no help in either assuring or destroying the hope of continuous persistence is here very important because, if reason would affirm that this hope "is wrecked in the theoretical reality,"[74] nothing but the blackest despair could ensue, and if it would affirm the contrary, the grant of such a certainty would remove the cause of the pain, removing at the same time the consciousness that was meant to be preserved, for only that which "feels, suffers, compassionates, loves and yearns, is consciousness."[75] Thus whatever solutions may be proposed must respect this total incompatibility with reason, if they are not to lead to a dissolution of the problem itself. The key to the solution is in feeling itself, in the maintenance of feeling, in its propagation, for all those who do not partake of it merely dream their life, they do not think, "what we ourselves call thinking."[76]

At the stage of the dream, therefore, all the tangibility that anyone possesses comes to him from the substantial existence of the conscious individual who dreams him: "when a man affirms his I, his personal consciousness, he affirms man, the concrete and real man, he affirms the true humanism—which is not that of the things of man, but that of man—and when he affirms man, he affirms consciousness. Because the unique consciousness of which we are conscious is that of man."[77] It is in this assertion that, at least in one corner, the dream is torn and some reality appears. This is rather a Leibnitzian conception which pictures each man, conscious or otherwise, as having "to live separated one from another, each one within his crust."[78] Consciousness is, therefore, the realization that such a crust exists; it is also the realization that the real is that of which one is conscious and not necessarily some class of objects defined objectively by reason. Whatever, in the crust, makes its presence known, exists:

41

Only by killing life, and the true truth with it, can one separate the historical hero from the fictional, the mystical, the fabulous, or the legendary, and claim that the one existed completely, or almost completely; the other, half so, and the one over there, in no way whatever: because to exist is to work, and who works exists.

To exist is to work, and Don Quixote, did he not work, and does he not work, in the mind as actively and as vividly as in his worked the knight-errants who had preceded him, as actively and as vividly as so many other heroes.[79]

From the point of view of the unique consciousness, what is here and now believed and lived is here and now real: the hallucination that makes someone call a hallucination what he hitherto believed is a misunderstanding of the nature of subjective truth. In subjective truth there is only a present belief which is believed and therefore subjectively true. It is only when some form of objectivity is given to the belief that it can retain some objective truth or falsity beyond the moment at which it is believed and lived. Therefore, "if Don Quixote works in those who know him works of life, Don Quixote is much more historical and real than so many men, pure names that pass in these chronicles;"[80] the "real" world and the world of "fiction" lose their distinction and "under these two worlds, supporting them, is another world, a substantial and eternal world in which I dream my self and those who have been—many still are—flesh of my mind and mind of my flesh, world of consciousness without space or time, in which lives, as a wave in the sea, the consciousness of my body."[81]

The most important single item in this "crust" is the very language which one uses, or rather, which one lives. It is a residue of lived experience, a philosophy, the strait jacket in which the lived experience takes shape, albeit an unfaithful one. It is a limitation as well as a tool because it has a tangibility and a resistance all its own. Therefore, it too serves to exacerbate the experience by never quite embodying it completely with life. And it has the ambiguous peculiarity of being both dependent and independent of each individual user: dependent, because, as any other item in the "crust," in order to exist subjectively, it must be experienced, it must work upon the consciousness; independent, because, so long as there are members in a linguistic group, the existence of the language will not depend upon that of any one specific member, as far as the group is concerned. There is, therefore, in language, a sort of parody of immortality, dependent in fact upon each user, but seemingly detached from any one. Conversely, there can be no consciousness unless it somehow expresses itself to itself with some symbolism or another, i.e., some language or another, for "language is what gives us the real, not as a mere vehicle of it, but as its true flesh, of which all the rest, the mute or inarticulate representation, is but the skeleton."[82] Consciousness, self-consciousness, is thought about one's own self, and "to think is for one to speak with his own self,"[83] is to give language substantial reality: "that the substance / of man is the word, and our triumph / to make the word our flesh."[84]

The question then arises, which aggravates still the feeling of intangibility and uncertainty at the origin of self-consciousness, as to what is in fact more real: the feeling which, as "skeleton," prompts the man to prop up the words this way and that in order to approximate his experience, or the words, once they are propped up and become, as it were, common property. Which is truly existing, the lone consciousness, or the various images that others may have as experienced denotations of the man's own name, and that name? "When a man, asleep and inert in bed, dreams something, what is it that exists most: he as a consciousness that dreams, or his dream?"[85] There is no answer to that question. All there is is the question. The solution given by Unamuno in *Paz en la Guerra*[86] in the final acquiescence of Pedro Antonio to *la condition humaine* should be considered as indicative, not of a position advocated by the author as *the* answer, but rather as what he would have liked to be able to believe, as well as what, realistically, a person of Pedro Antonio's character and background might be expected to believe.

The difference between the presentation of the credo of Pedro Antonio and that of Pachico, although they both agree in their contents, is here quite instructive. Pedro Antonio's is a quiet, unconscious assent to the world order; Pachico's is just as quiet, but it is conscious.[87] Pachico "contemplates"[87] and discovers; Pedro Antonio "lets himself be rocked, indifferent, in the routine cares of the day;" he "hopes that this deep life prolong itself for him beyond death, in order to enjoy, in a day without night, the perpetual light, . . . in imperturbable and secure peace, peace from within and from without." "Such hope is the reality which makes his life peaceful in the middle of his cares, and eternal within its brief, perishable course."[88] The emphasis should be placed here on the word "peaceful" which gives the clue to the fact that Pedro Antonio is not *self*-conscious, for if he were, in Unamuno's conception, his hope would have to be constantly renewed in fight. Although the difference between the two credos becomes apparent only in the light of later work, it is the first intimation of a double standard which has led

43

to many a confusion and is best symbolized by the two personalities of Sancho and Don Quixote. Don Quixote is self-conscious; Sancho is conscious.

The Sanchos, the Pedro Antonios, use language to transmit their ideas, as Schopenhauer's fools exchange their playing cards, according to the anecdote which Unamuno liked to repeat,[89] using words as ready-made instruments of exchange and unwittingly wearing them and marking them. It is through them and in them that language, the tradition of the community, its body, its matter, are transmitted which form the texture of the "crust" that emprisons the self-conscious individual. For "to think without knowing that one thinks, that is not to be one's own self, that is not to be one's self,"[90] and the Sanchos and the Pedro Antonios are not themselves, they simply are. They constitute "this world of the silent" in which lives "the true tradition, the eternal one, in the present, not in the past dead forever and buried in dead things."[91]

Thus, "In the soul of Spain live and work, besides our souls, those of all those who are living today, and perhaps more than these, the souls of all our forebears. Our own souls, those of those who are living today, are those which live least in them, because our souls do not enter that of our country until we have unfastened them, until after our temporal death."[92] In other words, considering for a moment as decided the question of relative reality in favor of the "crust" rather than the self-conscious being inside, all traces of all those who left their mark on the flesh of the nation by their thought, by their work, by their guidance or their folly, to such an extent that that thought is incorporated in manners of speech, customs, and reflex actions of the great body politic, these traces, through the present actions they have upon the consciousness of men, whether these men are conscious of it or not, in fact exist in a much more powerful and important manner than do the men themselves upon whom they act. And the same truth can be expressed from the point of view of the reality of the self-conscious being inside the crust, if one supposes that the question of reality should be decided in his favor. And Unamuno writes: "I carry within me all that which passed before me and with myself I perpetuate it, and perhaps it all goes in my seeds, and all my forebears live completely in me, and they will live, jointly with me, in my descendants."[93]

History, therefore, cannot be considered as a single linear progression going from "poor" to "perfect" in a continuous line of progress. History is all here and now. In a more or less distinct or occult manner, all the past is here upon us, living near us and in us and through us, present in the most modern discovery as well as in the most antiquated usage. Progress is not "a series of ascending undulations,"[94] it "is a series of qualitative expansions and concentrations, it is a self-enriching of the social environment in complexity, so that this complexity then condensates itself by organizing itself, descending in the eternal depths of Humanity, and thus facilitating a new progress: it is a self-succession of trees and seeds, each seed better than the preceding one, richer each tree than the one which preceded it."[94] Thus progress is a continuous refinement, or at least, Unamuno's denial of the adequacy of the "lineal conception,"[94] leaves no other choice of interpretation of his own schematization which might otherwise seem compatible with the lineal conception.

The important thing in such a conception of history is no longer the dreary recitation of wars and battles, the ghostly procession of period portraits, it is much more than this: it is the intimate scrutiny of a manner of life, the careful observation and understanding of the evolution of a way of life through the ages, because "All our history does not mean anything unless it can help us to understand better how the Spanish peasant lives and dies today, how he uses the earth he plows and how he pays his lease, and in what state of mind he receives the last sacraments."[95] It is what is subjectively true here and now, what is lived here and now, that is important and which must be, *tant bien que mal*, approximated, because it is what is now actually lived by all, directly or indirectly, consciously or otherwise, it is what in fact forms the crust which surrounds the self-conscious individual, the flesh of his dream, if it is all a dream.

For the question still remains. Though the anguished eye of consciousness may in turn give life and tangibility to various aspects of its crust, the ultimate question has not as yet been answered. And the two possible solutions which first present themselves, each one exclusive of the other, irritate but fail to satiate the desire for life of the sentient man. The first of these is what one might call the "solipsist" solution, according to which the only thing that does give reality to the dream is the sentient self-consciousness and nothing else. This has already been noted as unsatisfactory, but, the following text specifies better the sentient basis of the refutation, as against others which might be rooted in reasons and facts:

My legend! My novel! That is to say the legend, the novel that of me, Miguel de Unamuno, the one whom we call thus, we have conjointly made, the others and I, my friends and my enemies, and

45

my friendly I and my enemy I. And I have here why I cannot look at myself an instant in the mirror, because immediately my eyes elude me through my eyes, through their picture, and the minute I look at my gaze I feel myself emptying myself of my own self, lose my history, my legend, my novel, return to the unconscious, to the past, to nothingness.[96]

The second solution is diametrically opposed to that one: "If the representations that of myself— . . . —have A, B, C, D, E, etc., were fused into a compound representation in the manner of Galton's compound photographs, this compound and collective representation, with its nimbus of contradictions would be more the I that I am myself than the one that I imagine myself to be; it would be my historical I, my extrinsic personality, the role that I represent in our little world."[97] Either "everything lives inside Consciousness, my Consciousness,"[98] or we must "submerge ourselves in the soul of the mountain, in the soul of the lake, in the soul of the people of the village, lose ourselves in it in order to remain in it,"[99] such is the dilemma.

The first answer represents almost the traditional Idealist position as expressed by Berkeley, for example in *The Principles of Human Knowledge;*[100] the other, its contrary, might be construed as representing a form of the realist position if careful emphasis is placed upon the fact that Unamuno selects for his metaphor words denoting common or objective things liable to be observed and testified to by more than one person. Implied in this formulation is the permanence of some form of reality independent of any one specific human existence and in which in turn any such human existence finds both support and place.

That neither answer be satisfactory is stated by Unamuno when he asserts, "Philosophy is the human product of each philosopher."[101] The choice between these two solutions is not a matter of distinguishing an objective truth, but a matter of expressing that which one would rather live, a solipsist or monadic world, or a realist or positivist world. In this light, neither answer can satisfy the yearning for certainty and continued existence of the sentient self-consciousness, since, reciprocally, they demonstrate each other to be gratuitous acts of volition and not demonstration. Thus the actual problem is beyond the dilemma, underlying it as it were, and concerns in fact the reality of the only certitude which the Unamunian *cogito* gives, namely, the present, felt pain which the sentient being calls his self. A rapid circular investigation as to what all does constitute this "self" or may seem to do so, leads therefore to no comfort whatever, to no solution whatever, aggravating, if anything, the original uncertainty with respect to the nature and the duration of that "self" suddenly revealed. Is life "a joke?"[102] Is it but a game of the gods, "so that the coming generations will have something to sing?"[103] "Is all of this anything more than a dream within another dream?"[104] Are all men "fictional beings" doomed to die when God "will stop to dream them?"[105] These questions have to be answered still, all that the Quixotic Weltanschauung shows is that the self-conscious man, a sentient question-mark, and the universe in the center of which he finds himself, are indissolubly bound. "What is the end of the whole Universe?"[106] and "What is the intimate reality of a man?"[107] are two different facets of the same question, namely, "What am I, as a self-conscious being, as the self-conscious being of which I have total certainty, doing here, and for how long will I remain, if I remain?".

5. "QUIXOTIC" EXISTENTIALISM
Part 2: Agonistic Ethics

In the best whodunit tradition, the hero, coming to his senses and finding himself bound and gagged in a dark place, silently asks himself: "Where am I?" and then: "What am I doing here?" Sooner or later, he is provided with the answers, and the author ends the book, and the reader can turn to other things. The conscious, that is, self-conscious man, according to Unamuno, finds himself in a similar situation, with the notable exception that the answer is long in coming and that he hopes that it will never completely come. For the Unamunian hero, the bittersweet realization of his own presence is clouded mercifully by the infinitely more bitter realization of his own gratuity. Unlike Hollywood detectives he finds himself neither essential nor immortal and, on the contrary, vulnerable and in deadly danger. His presence is not necessitated by anything he can imagine, not even the plot, and his absence would seemingly not ruffle any too radically the existing order of things such as it appears to him. It is a frightfully depressing situation which is made all the more depressing by the fact that the other protagonists seem unaware that anything is amiss and go on quietly through their intended parts as oxen pass through the slaughterhouse. He would, perhaps, like to be able to do likewise, or, on the contrary, prefer to remain aware of his presence even at the cost of his tranquillity. And he might, being aware, attempt to make others aware also, or remain content to sit back and watch them come and go, dead crusts made to carry a burden which they don't even feel. Or, unable to remain consistently upon the same path, he may in turn agonizingly reappraise each decision, remaining aware, painfully aware of his own presence to himself, and remaining unable to take either comfort or despair in this awareness. Last but not least, he may even wonder about the quality of his awareness and ask himself if this too is not but a role assigned to him by the author of the novel, a burden he is made to carry, or, rather, the evidence of some unknown burden he is made to carry. In short, he may ask himself if this too is not but an illusion.

This is the crux of the Unamunian problem. It is to a despaired analysis of this sort that Unamuno refers when he writes: "I have come to know a terrible sickness similar in the order of the mind to what, in the order of matter, would be an autophagy, an ulcerated stomach which, destroying the epithelium, begins to digest itself."[1] And the abyss of despair into which he is then plunged knows no bounds: "It is, in fact, a terrible thing when, touching the 'vanity of vanities!' all beauty loses its attractiveness and all impression its savor, when one reaches the painful obsession of the desert, which makes us kill the hours, and unites us in the sadness of the uselessness of all effort, when, the appetite for life having been extinguished, one lives as by necessity, by routine, by cowardice or by fear of death."[2] It is then that the very uncertainty which caused the despair in the first place, is seen as merciful, as a grace, because it leaves open the chance that, rather than "vanity of vanities!" all be plenitude, that there be a rhyme and a reason to this awareness.

The first step, therefore, is to be aware of the "mystery," to know that there is a problem, because only through this knowledge can one be self-conscious and therefore exist at least in one's own eyes. It is the presence of the mystery, its existence in the consciousness, the fact that it is at work there and provokes feelings and thoughts, which is pain, the root of consciousness itself.[3] The unique present moment of consciousness is a continuous confrontation in which the sentient man repeats: "I do not know, that is sure; possibly, I will never be able to know, but I 'want' to know. I want it, and that is enough,"[4] and this sentence is not the expression of a determination, it is a description of a state in which the man finds himself. "Want" is here made to denote a state of need, of physical as well as mental need. The consciousness is consciousness of the pain caused by the experience of want which is the experience of life itself.

For this want to remain it must be continuously dissatisfied for if the mystery were ever solved the solution would immediately sap the basis for self-consciousness, namely the pain caused by the want. In order that the want may be continuously dissatisfied the need must continuously be felt and the attempts at an answer must exacerbate it continuously rather than discourage it. In other words the result must be the emphasis of two things: first, the continued subjective truth of the need; second, the demonstrated inadequacy of reason in the matter. Thus the objective part of the criterion of truth is nullified and the subjective part is continuously shown to be the sole adequate criterion. If reason were shown in some ways to be adequate, then its solution, whatever it might be, would become liable to subjective evidence as well as objective evidence, thus adequately replacing the mere want and effectively annihilating the consciousness of it, that is to say the self-consciousness. And in order that the want be continuously fed,

49

continuous attempts at satisfying it must be made which reason must be consistently recognizing as "lacking all sense," as being absurd, not true, not false, not right, not wrong, but absurd,[5] that is to say, not just irrational, but "anti-rational."[6] It is in love and through love that the anti-rational knowledge is acquired, a revelation of both uniqueness and being.[7]

The self-conscious individual will be conscious of being conscious of being in love; he will wonder as to the nature and the object of such love and attempt to save the experience of it in its uniqueness. Thus, if we look upon the self-conscious being as the center of a monad-like area of which he is conscious of being conscious, love makes known to him the existence of another such sentient and conscious being, and this knowledge is neither rational nor rationally warranted, it is the immediate, subjective, experiential certainty of another existence, of another consciousness of pain, solitary and unique to itself until it too, through love and compassion, gets the revelation of another's suffering, that is to say of another's existence.[8]

Unamuno puts into the feeling, or drive, or vital force he denotes by "love" all the emotions, all the striving, all the need and the desire as various nouns expressing the same irritated need, striving and willing and wanting. This elemental force, which to him is at the root of being and perhaps is all that being in fact really is, through love turns upon itself and recognizes its own self, first in "these little things"[9] in order to end "compassionating all."[10] That is to say that the solitary consciousness a transient being has of itself, as if a wave upon the sea would suddenly become aware of itself as a wave, and would then become dimly aware of the immensity of the sea of which it is but a ripple, that solitary consciousness is the first glimpse of an immensity of being of which it is but a wave. For the self which compassionates itself upon becoming self-conscious is no less real, and no more so, than whatever else is compassionated by the sentient consciousness. Thus from one object of love, love grows to another and yet another, becoming stronger as it grows, and more demanding, until it compassionates everything, personalizing all.[11] That is why from the consciousness "that one has of one's own radical nothingness," "one gathers new forces with which to aspire to be all."[12]

It is this movement, this present constant aspiration, that is love, or need, or pain through lack, that is being in the Unamunian sense; it is this ever present aspiration, unchanging perception of time, unmoved present observation of a continuing future, unending, unsatiated present desire for a continuing future, that is the inner reality of a "man of flesh and bone," that is the inner reality of a man, "be he of those that they call fiction, which is the same."[13] It is this desire, embodied momentarily and continuously in words expressing what one honestly subjectively believes to be one's present goal, which is "the creator, and is truly the real" self,[14] for "love hopes, hopes always, without ever wearying of hoping."[15] And it may be worth noting here again the fortunate ambiguity of the Spanish language which preserves the sentient or felt aspect of the ideas, and in this case uses the same word, *esperar,* to mean both to hope and to wait, in this way preserving all the anguished waiting that is hope, even the most radiant hope.

The shift of emphasis from the self-conscious being looking upon himself as he is, to the same being, through love, hoping to become what he would like to be, is the lesson of the Unamunian *cogito,* and the lesson of the sentience, of the vital force which the *cogito* reveals. It is fully consistent with the Unamunian affirmation that "to exist is to work,"[16] because the future, or rather the goal toward which one tends, by the mere fact that one now tends toward it, now is at work within one's life and therefore exists. It is also consistent with the subjective criterion of truth, since it is that which is now subjectively lived and believed in the sense Unamuno specifies time and again for those terms. It does not fall under the sway of the objective criterion of truth since it is not a matter of rational proof but solely a matter of present belief. Taking the anecdote which Poincaré related as a case in point, one can say that the solution to the Fuschian functions, which Poincaré was trying to prove, was, while he was trying to prove it—i.e., to show that it satisfied also the objective criterion of truth—already subjectively true and his goal: the reality of Henri Poincaré then, was Poincaré as the discoverer of the solution of this mathematical problem because it was a reality which was then at work in and through Poincaré. If Poincaré had not succeeded in solving that problem, that would not have changed anything in the reality which he had just lived and its truth while he was living it. Only, at the precise moment at which he would have started to live the idea that he had failed, and that idea had existed in him and through him by working upon him, coordinating his actions—i.e., moving him dejectedly to put down his pencil, tear the paper, turn to another task—at that moment the previous goal would no longer have been subjectively true. But for the passing while of a present moment, it would have been. And that is the important thing, because the fact that one such goal fails only when it is replaced by another only demonstrates

51

the unavoidability of "having a goal" and, in an indirect way, proves the exactness of Unamuno's assertion. Finally, whatever goal one may take, unless it can be demonstrated beyond a doubt that it "fails in the theoretical reality,"[17] and thus one can do away with it, if the theoretical reality has nothing to say in the matter, then the goal may remain subjectively true as long as it pleases the individual. This is the hidden key to Unamuno's "irrationalism," as it has been called mistakenly:[18] not that one should follow his every whim unreservedly and uncritically, and thus consecrate the failure of reason, but that reason itself is a guide which enables one to distinguish between that upon which it has jurisdiction and that upon which it does not: it is, in fact, irrational or unreasonable, not to recognize that "reason can only work upon the irrational."[19]

"And it is through the one that we wanted to be, not through the one that we have been, that we will be saved or that we will be lost."[20] For it is that which we want that is operative in our subjective reality, not that which has been or that which is: "Neither the past can be more than as it has been, nor is it possible that the present be more than the way it is; (the future) can be always future."[21] And it is, in fact, the future that is lived here and now, "the true future is today,"[22] because it is here and now that the want and the need are lived, and that, in that way, the future is created.

Thus, what gives finality to the being is the being himself; he is the one who wants and thus creates his own reality. Whether he be conscious of doing so or not, the man conscious of a goal gives reality to that goal merely by striving for it, independently of the actual success of his endeavor. "That which we call reality, is it anything else than an illusion which prompts us to work and produce works? The practical effect of any vision is the only valid one."[23] And the practical effect is not the end product, but simply the present exertion independent of its outcome. After all, the outcome, whatever it may be, is past the minute it is reached and immediately becomes supplanted by another goal, or be it another reality. Those who insist upon its paramount importance are like "a traveller insisting on denying the road that remains to be travelled over by him, and in holding as true and certain only the road already covered."[24] Even the explorer of virgin territories will concede that the unknown ahead is, in its present lure and ominousness, more real to him than the country already explored which no longer bears any present menace. Or if it does, it is still in the future, and, figuratively, also on a road as yet untraveled.

52

The simply conscious being, therefore, is the being conscious of a goal, the one who does not say: "I have come to do thus and so," but in fact does thus and so; the self-conscious being is the one who can say: "I have come to do thus and so." He is the hero, the one who affirms: "I know whom I want to be."[25] He is the one who asserts: "I have come to realize myself."[26] He is the one who knows that the world is "for consciousness,"[27] that "man is an end, not a means,"[28] that "the whole civilization addresses itself to man, to each man, to each I."[28] "Consciousness and finality are the same thing, at bottom,"[29] and this finality is the one desired, the one which is real in the life of the conscious man.

It is this reality through lack, this presence by absence, so to speak, which is the fundamental step from the Unamunian *cogito*: "Distressed when we feel that everything passes, that we ourselves pass, that that which is ours passes, that all that which surrounds us passes, the anguish reveals to us the consolation of that which does not pass, of the eternal and of the beautiful."[30] Understand: distressed upon seeing that everything passes, we feel through this distress the need for the eternal, the permanent, and this feeling of need, of want, when it is exacerbated to the paroxysm of a vital desire is the love of something eternal and permanent, the revelation of something eternal and permanent. This is properly the Unamunian "leap," but it is a leap that is not made eyes closed and unknowingly: Unamuno continuously stresses the importance of the desire and of the pain. Consciousness is consciousness of pain, love and pain are the same mystery, and "only those are saved who desired to save themselves, only those become eternal who lived afflicted of a terrible hunger for eternity and for eternization."[31] To be is to want to be, not just this or that, as one becomes a doctor or a television repairman, but to be absolutely and irreplaceably, and not just another of a kind.

That is the anguish behind Unamuno's vehement protest: "I do not want to let myself be classified:"[32] that is the goal of consciousness: to be, continuously, unique and irreplaceable. And from this goal comes the constant need to feel and to perceive, to be conscious of being conscious: the conscious being cannot allow himself to fall into the trap of routine and sleep. He must always perceive his limits, he must always be conscious, and to be conscious of anything is to apprehend it, not as a dream, but as a being, separate, similar yet unique, and this can only be done through love. The conscious being must, therefore, attempt to love all, "to personalize all,"[33] and the consciousness must ever strive to "universalize itself."[34] "It is necessary to spiritualize everything":[35]

53

Love personalizes that which it loves. The only way to be in love with an idea is to personalize it. And when the love is so great and so vivid, and so strong and overflowing that it loves everything, then it personalizes everything and discovers that the Total All, that the Universe, is also a Person who has a Consciousness, Consciousness which in its turn suffers, sympathizes and loves; that is to say, is Consciousness. And this Consciousness of the Universe, which love discovers personalizing all it loves, is that which we call God. And thus the soul sympathizes with God and feels itself being pitied by Him, loves Him and feels itself being loved by Him, sheltering its misery amid the eternal and infinite misery, which is, by being eternized and infinitated, the supreme happiness itself.

God is, then, the personalization of Everything, He is the eternal and infinite Consciousness of the Universe, Consciousness caught in matter and fighting in order to liberate itself from it. We personalize All in order to save ourselves from nothingness, and the only mystery truly mysterious is that of pain.[36]

This total aspiration, uncompromising and raw, can be viewed also from the other pole, from the God which is thus created, being believed and lived. And from this point of view, the unique consciousness aspiring merely to be, is but "the projection of God in the finite,"[37] and all human history, and all the history of the life of any one man, is but a dream of God,[38] and the changes throughout the ages of the shapes of animals is but an indication that God "has changed style."[39]

But, just as Unamuno, author, and Augusto Pérez, his creature, arguing as to who was the real being and who the dream, could not come to agreement,[40] so is it impossible to decide in favor of either God or the man he dreams separately. "God and man create each other mutually; in fact God makes himself and reveals himself in man, and man makes himself in God; God made himself his own self."[41] Thus, if the Unamunian "leaps," as from the consciousness of lack to the interpretation of that lack as the manifestation in the sentience of that which would eradicate it by its presence, are accepted, they cannot be taken as a demonstrated certainty or as Unamuno's affirmation of a statement of fact which he would be prepared to defend as that which in fact is, but rather they must be interpreted as a statement of belief. They constitute what Unamuno would wish to know to be the case, but in truth does not. The Unamunian "leap" is a clearly recognized act of faith, and faith, according to Saint Paul in a definition endorsed by Unamuno is " 'the substance of the things that are hoped (expected), the demonstration of that which is not seen.' "[42]

However, this "faith," this "God," are not to be construed as excuses for one's own failures, they cannot be so construed because they are not "known" with certainty. When Don Juan Tenorio exclaims: "Of my steps upon the earth, Heaven answers and not I!"[43] he is overlooking the fact that this Heaven he so glibly invokes is just as much his own creation as any other thought of his, or any one of his decisions, and therefore, to discharge upon It the responsibility of his own steps is subreptitiously to deceive himself and leave that one cardinal step unaccounted for. On the other hand, to the man who refuses to ascribe the responsibility of his own actions to any otherworldly agency, but needs that otherworldly agency in order to feel that his agonized endorsement of his own acts is not so much senseless effort, his obvious part in fostering this witness of his path upon the earth will cause him enough anguish to make him realize just how fundamentally this God is essential to him, and just how unreasonable and unwarranted an assumption it is to postulate Him. "It is not so much, Nicodemus, that the good be good because they believe, nor the bad, bad for lack of faith, but that by being good those that are good believe, and by not being good, those that are bad do not."[44] "The good man cannot resign himself to being wasted,"[45] and he can't either let himself be lulled into a false certainty.

His faith, therefore, is not the belief in "what we did not see,"[46] it is the creation of "what we do not see."[46] "To create what we do not see, yes, to create it, and to live it, and to consume it, and to create it again and to consume it anew, living it another time, in order to create it another time . . . and thus in an incessant vital anguish."[47] Thus this God, when the yearning is so great that His absence seems impossible, bursts into emptiness like a soap bubble at the first prick of reason and needs must be re-created through the affirmation of an intolerable want, born anew and again almost satiated but never quite totally so. Formulated in terms of the theory of language, this constant movement from the absolute certainty of the experience to the total inadequacy of the residual expression in which it culminates, illustrates the fundamental inadequacy of the frozen symbol and can be summed up by saying that "God is indefinable":[48] "To want to define God is to pretend to limit Him in our mind, that is to say, to kill Him."[48]

Yet, faith is knowing, to believe is a form of knowing, "even if it is no other thing than to know our vital desire and up to formulating it."[49] And this formulation must be nothing else but subjectively true, since its very object is indefinable. "Faith is, then, the creative power, flower

55

of the will, and its office is to create,"[50] to create the words, the expressions, the ideas which will partially salvage the reality of the experience believed, that is to say, the future longed and hoped for, which, being experienced, lives in the conscious man. Of these expressions, of this experience, only the sentient man can affirm the sincerity; therefore, "faith is, above all, sincerity, tolerance and compassion,"[51] and no one may condemn any faith, "when it is spontaneous and simple, even though it may see itself forced to pour itself in forms that deform it. Every faith is sacred. The faith of fetichism is so, which inspires, advises, gives strengths, instills courage, makes miracles."[52]

This God, thus created through the continuity of a momentary belief in the soul and the flesh of one man, is the eternal, immortal being in whom the unique remains forever unique and forever true. When Augusto Pérez tells Unamuno that "one does not dream twice the same dream,"[53] he is in fact telling him that the most fleeting instant during which a goal is lived remains forever the same in the eternal Consciousness of God, "for Whom yesterday and tomorrow are always today."[54] "Nothing passes, nothing is dissipated, nothing is annihilated; the smallest particle of matter, the weakest knock of a force are eternized, and there is no vision, however fleeting it may be, which does not remain forever reflected in some part."[55] "The temporal world has roots in eternity, and there yesterday is joined with today and tomorrow."[56] And this eternity is the eternal Consciousness of God, which incessantly is dreamed to dream the world, by the faithful, those who "desired to be saved."

It is this world which is substantial: "The dream is that which is life, reality, creation. Faith itself is nothing but, according to Saint Paul, the substance of the things which are hoped for, and that which is hoped for is a dream. And faith is the source of reality, because it is life. To believe is to create."[57] And in what it has of aesthetic feeling, this faith leads us to the work of art. "In the art, in fact, we search for a parody of eternization. If, in the beautiful, the mind a moment becomes calm, and relaxes and recovers, although its anguish is not cured, it is because the beautiful is the revelation of the eternal, of the divine of things, and beauty is nothing but the perpetuation of instantaneity. For just as truth is the end of rational knowledge, beauty is the end of hope, perhaps irrational at bottom."[58] Beauty, thus understood, is practically synonymous with subjective truth, just as the word "truth" as used above is synonymous with objective truth. "The beautiful is the superfluous, that which has its end in itself; the flower of life."[59]

56

And the goal that a man lives at any one time, the real goal, not the one he may profess to live, is the one that has its end in itself. The Unamunian "leap" shifts the importance from what is actually done, to what is wanted. What becomes the real and the eternal is that which is lived, is the goal, each goal of each man at each time of his life, no matter how fleeting, how inconspicuous it may have been even to himself. For if the postulated God is, then "nothing is annihilated." Thus the important thing is not the actual performance, but the intention, at every moment. "Time is irreversible. If you take a path, you close all the others to yourself."[60] "You are a slave in your acts, but not in your intentions."[61] If anyone retorts that, if all this is truly a dream of God, then we are in fact not responsible even for our intentions, the reply is that we do not know if it really is, and that the act of postulating such a Weltanschauung is itself to be judged according to the intention one has in doing it: the intention, therefore, precedes even this fundamental act. This awareness of his own intentions is the appanage of the self-conscious man. Thus again, at the basis, surges the vital desire which prompted the whole anguished research in the first place, for at the beginning is the intention, that is, the irrepressible desire of the self-conscious man to remain aware and self-conscious, "To be, to be always and without end!"[62]

And this desire can only be felt when there is doubt, when it is not satisfied; therefore, Unamuno writes:

> I want to establish that uncertainty, doubt, the perpetual fight of our final destiny, mental despair, and the lack of solid and stable dogmatic foundation, can be the basis of ethics.
>
> He who bases or believes that he bases his conduct—internal or external, of sentiment or of action—in a dogma or theoretical principle which he considers incontrovertible, runs the risk of making a fanatic of himself, and furthermore, on the day in which this dogma breaks in his hands, or loosens, his ethics loosen. . . .
>
> But he who believes that he navigates, perhaps even without a course, in a fickle and sinkable raft, does not have to be moved by the fact that the raft moves under his feet and threatens to founder. This one believes that he works, not because he thinks his principle of action true, but in order to make it so, in order to prove its truth, in order to create for himself his own spiritual world.
>
> My conduct has to be the best proof, the moral proof, of my supreme desire.[63]

And if that supreme desire is the continuous survival or persistence of

57

one's own self, not just of one's own soul but of one's own body or "perispirit" as well,[64] then the actions that one performs must make him indispensable, must warrant this persistence of being. "Martyrdom makes the faith, and not the faith the martyrdom."[65] And, if God exists, this is another way to present the problem: "All your problem is this: whether you have to blur your idea and erase it and make it so that God forgets you, or whether you have to sacrifice yourself to it and make it float and live forever in the eternal and infinite Consciousness of the Universe. Either God or oblivion."[66] But, since Unamuno does not feel warranted in asserting either that God exists or that He does not, since, in fact, the behavior of any man is his subjective proof of the genuineness of the beliefs or faith he professes, perhaps the best formulation of Unamuno's ethics of uncertainty is his modification of Sénancour's sentence,[67] changing it from the negative to the positive: " 'And if nothingness is what is in store for us, let us make this an injustice.' "[68]

The only way to make it an injustice is to follow the precept of Saint Paul: " 'Be perfect as your Heavenly Father is perfect,' "[69] for "He who does not aspire to the impossible will scarcely do anything that is worth while."[69] And the only way to be so perfect, or to begin to attempt it, is to be sincere, and to strive "to be all, to be I, and to be everyone of the others, it is to be Humanity, to be Universe. And there is no other way to be all the others than to give oneself to all, and when everything will be in everything, everything will be in each one of us. The apocatastasis is more than a mystic dream, it is a norm of action, a beacon of high deeds."[70] For to keep on being conscious one must continuously "augment consciousness,"[71] that is to say, continuously sympathize with everything, know everything, through love. To be perfect means, therefore, to attempt to be all in the sense of being conscious of each by compassionating each and therefore losing one's self in the pain of each and being conscious of doing so. Since consciousness is consciousness of limitation, is pain caused by the existence of something which limits one's own being, the dual movement of immersion in the pain of another and in one's own pain at not being the other but at being limited by him can be pictured either as leaving "in all, imperishable, our emblem,"[72] or as expressing one's self, manifesting one's self, revealing one's self such as one is—or such as one wants to be—that is to say, as being perfect or accomplished in each moment.[73]

For the consciousness of another being is shock, but it is mutual shock, and therefore mutual pain, and the self-conscious man consciously imposes his being on the other, forcing the other to become conscious of it, and doing so, the self-conscious man continues to be conscious, furthers his self-consciousness, and therefore reveals himself to himself as he is, and is perfect and accomplished at every moment that he so does. But, imposing his presence in this way, the self-conscious man gives pain, surging as a limit in front of the merely conscious man, thus, contributing to the extent of his power to the birth of another self-consciousness, if it should arise, and to that extent "proving his faith by his conduct." In a similar way, the self-conscious man who feels the pain of being of a thing, even a star,[74] performs the one act by which he imposes himself on that thing, the one act which may lead to the birth of consciousness, the one act which is proof of his will to have faith.

The self-conscious men, the Don Quixotes, the heroes,[75] the great hermits,[76] the geniuses,[76] "carry a whole society within themselves."[76] They are "the individualized multitude,"[76] "the people made person,"[76] "the collective soul individualized."[77] They carry within themselves all that of which they are conscious of being conscious, that is to say, all the experience of a people as distilled in its words, symbols, traditions, and which they make their own, using it, vivifying it. Language, this strait jacket within which the conscious man salvages his transient self, becomes to the self-conscious man more than a tool, a guide, a staff with which to strike the rock in order to make spurt the living water of consciousness. And the self-conscious men need the rock, the Sanchos, for they need limits to be conscious, they need the dead weight of the people to make them see the windmills through the giants, just as the Sanchos need the Quixotes to learn to see the giants through the windmills, so that neither can ever bask in the traitorous certainty of his own opinion, and both can live in vivifying doubt, the Sanchos "Sanchopancizing" the Quixotes, the Quixotes "Quixotizing" the Sanchos.[78] This fight, this constant striving to found on bases of rock the faith which continuously founders, this is the continuous death of the consciousness which, instantaneous phoenix, immediately reborn of this fire starts again to burn anew—"those who do not die, do not live; those who do not die at each instant in order to resuscitate immediately do not live, and those who do not doubt, do not believe"[79]—pursuing its own dream of being and thus being, for "to be is to want to be."[80]

This priority of the intention over the actual act raises a question which Unamuno considered as "the Achilles argument"[81] against his agonistic ethics, or ethics of fight. This argument is the one which stems from the "necessity to do that which bears no excuse,"[81] that is to say, to perform an irreparable act which may not seem to follow the "accepted" morality. Unamuno counters it with Don Quixote's famous reply to those importuning questions about the certainty of his conviction that he was bewitched: "I know and hold true for myself that I am bewitched, and this suffices for the security of my conscience."[81] Unamuno puts the emphasis upon "for the security of my conscience," because, at the bottom of any decision, no one ever decides but that he does not know whether in his heart and conscience his decision is conforming with his intimate conviction on the matter. Since the basis of Unamuno's ethics is the intention, if the intention be good, let him cast the first stone who feels a superior wisdom, but not at the man, rather at the man's stupidity, for the man did only as best he could if he acted "for the security of his conscience."

Thus, in a world of flux, uncertainty and death, Unamuno proclaims the motive to life of the human self-consciousness, its mission being to give finality and eternity to the Universe, personalizing it in a God of pain and sorrow, in a God of love. For "God is the love which saves"[82] and that love, which is God, is borne in human hearts. And Unamuno demands that those who are awake awake the sleeping, that those who are self-conscious turn others towards their own selves, and, discovering what they want to be, do as Alonso Quijano, sally forth to live their faith: "And thus, Don Quixote, descendant of himself, was born in spirit when he decided himself to go forth in search of adventures, and gave himself a new name, on account of the prowesses which he thought to carry out successfully."[83]

NOTES

Introduction

1. Gonzales Caminero, Nemesio, S. I., *Trayectoria de su ideología y de su crisis religiosa,* v. I of the series *Unamuno* (Comillas, Santander: Universidad Pontificia, 1948), 227. (No subsequent volume is as yet available.)

2. Unamuno, Miguel de, *Obras Completas* (Madrid: A. Aguado, 1951-52). 5 vols. published to date; I, 88, *Recuerdos de Niñez y de Mocedad.*

3. Unamuno, OC, I, 1, *Recuerdos de Niñez y de Mocedad.*

4. García Blanco, Manuel, *Crónica Unamuniana, Cuadernos de la Cátedra Miguel de Unamuno, No. 1* (Salamanca: Universidad de Salamanca, Facultad de Filosofía y Letras, 1948), p. 104.

5. Madariaga, Salvador de, "L'oeuvre et la figure de M. de Unamuno," *Europe,* VIII (Paris, 1925), 482.

6. Ferrater Mora, José, *M. de Unamuno: Bosquejo de una Filosofía* (Buenos Aires: Editorial Losada, 1944), pp. 34-5.

7. Torre, Guillermo de, *Tríptico del Sacrificio* (Buenos Aires: Editorial Losada, 1948), pp. 12-15.

8. Marías, Julián, *Filosofía Actual y Existencialismo en España* (Madrid: Revista de Occidente, 1955), p. 109.

9. Benítez, Hernán, *El Drama Religioso de Unamuno y Cartas a J. Ilundain* (Buenos Aires: Universidad de Buenos Aires, Instituto de Publicaciones, 1949), p. 141.

10. Cf., for example, I. M. Bocheński, *Contemporary European Philosophy,* trans. from the German (Berkeley and Los Angeles: University of California Press, 1956), p. 155, in which the author rejects the "Spanish critic" Unamuno, showing by this misnomer that he has either not read Unamuno or willfully taken an unwarranted view, as his note 5, p. 154, would lead one to believe. F. Copleston, S.J., *Contemporary Philosophy* (London: Burns and Oates, 1956), p. 143, remarks that "The number of people who give any real consideration to the problems which plagued, say, Kierkegaard or Unamuno, is limited." And the same kind of thing occurs in J. Marías, *Historia de la Filosofía* (2ª ed. ampliada; Madrid: Revista de Occidente, 1943), p. 316, and in P. Dominguez, *Historia de la Filosofía* (Madrid: 1942), as quoted by F. Meyer in *L'Ontologie de M. de Unamuno* (Paris: Presses Universitaires de France, 1955), p. ix, note 1.

11. Frischl, Johann, *Geschichte der Philosophie,* (Graz-Wien-Köln: Verlag Styria, 1954), Bd. V, pp. 67 seq., and p. 254.

12. Cf. in *Storia della Filosofia,* Cornelio Fabro, ed. (Roma: Coletti, 1954), part IV, 2d sec., by Michele F. Sciacca, who considers Unamuno as the proponent of a "pragmatismo 'Umanista,' " as against the "pragmatismo 'cosista' " of the American School; pp. 615 seq.

13. Meyer, *op. cit.*

14. Oromí, M., *Pensamiento Filosófico de M. de Unamuno* (Madrid: Espasa-Calpe, 1943).

15. Ceñal Lorente, Ramón, "La Filosofía Española Contemporánea," *Actos del primer congreso nacional de Filosofía,* Mendoza, Argentina, Marzo 30-Abril 9, 1949 (Universidad Nacional de Cuyo), I, 439: "if, by 'philosopher' is meant the technician and the systemizer who constructs with rigorous architecture a doctrinal edifice exclusively scientific in both content and form, it is certain that Unamuno was not a philosopher. But if he was not one in this sense,

it can be well ascertained that he really was one in another, much superior sense, since all his being, all his own humanity was itself all philosophy and problem in live flesh."

16. Meyer, *op. cit.*, p. xi, note 2, quoting from J. Kessel's *Die Grundstimmung in M. de Unamunos Lebens-philosophie* (Thesis, Bonn, 1937).

17. Unamuno, OC, III, 993, *Soliloquio.*

18. *Idem*, OC, IV, 695, *Del Sentimiento.*

19. *Idem*, OC, III, 593, *Ramplonería!*

20. Marías, *Historia de la Filosofía*, p. 316.

21. Niedermeyer, F., *Unamuno hier und heute* (Nürnberg: Glock und Lutz, 1956), p. 8.

22. Valbuena Prat, Angel, and Saz, Augustin del, *Historia de la Literatura Española* (siglos XVIII-XX), (2 ed.; Barcelona: Editorial Juventud, S. A., 1947), p. 118.

Chapter 1

1. Unamuno, OC, IV, 705, *Del Sentimiento.*
2. *Idem*, OC, III, 10, *En Torno al Casticismo.*
3. *Idem*, OC, III, 1187, *Un Filósofo del Sentido Común.*
4. *Idem*, OC, III, 9, *En Torno al Casticismo.*
5. *Idem*, OC, III, 461, *Intellectualidad y Espiritualidad.*
6. *Idem*, OC, III, 994, *Soliloquio.*
7. *Idem*, OC, IV, 704, *Del Sentimiento.*
8. *Idem*, OC, III, 506, *Plenitud de Plenitudes y Todo Plenitud!*
9. *Idem*, OC, IV, 705, *Del Sentimiento.*
10. *Ibid.*, p. 704.
11. *Ibid.*, p. 705.
12. *Ibid.*, p. 481.
13. *Idem*, OC, III, 705, *Qué es Verdad?*
14. *Idem*, Soneto 44: "La Palabra," *Rosario de Sonetos Líricos,* (Madrid: A. Aguado, 1950), p. 65.
15. *Idem*, OC, III, 1187, *Un Filósofo del Sentido Común.*
16. *Idem*, OC, IV, 724, *Aforismos y Definiciones.*
17. *Idem*, OC, III, p. 218, *La Ideocracia.*
18. *Idem*, OC, IV, 533; also, *ibid.*, p. 376, and III, 504-5, for example.
19. *Idem*, OC, IV, 461, *Del Sentimiento*: "the concrete substantive;" also, *idem*, I, 163, *De mi país*: "in the most concrete meaning of that word."
20. *Idem*, OC, I, 120, *Recuerdos de Niñez y Mocedad.*
21. *Idem*, OC, IV, 533, *Del Sentimiento.*
22. *Idem*, OC, I, 163, *De mi país*, "For me the Fatherland, in the most concrete meaning of that word, the sensible Fatherland—by opposition to the intellective, or even sentimental—".
23. *Idem*, OC, IV, 376, *Vida de Don Quijote y Sancho.*
24. *Idem*, OC, III, 504, *Plenitud de Plenitudes y Todo Plenitud!*
25. *Idem*, OC, IV, 912, *Como Se Hace Una Novela.*
26. *Idem*, OC, IV, 760, *Alrededor del Estilo.*
27. *Idem*, OC, III, 506, *Plenitud de Plenitudes y Todo Plenitud!*
28. *Idem*, OC, IV, 206-7, *Vida de Don Quijote y Sancho.*
29. *Idem*, OC, III, 9, *En Torno al Casticismo.*
30. *Idem*, OC, III, 506, *Plenitud de Plenitudes y Todo Plenitud!*
31. *Idem*, OC, III, 117, *La Enseñanza del Latín en España.*
32. *Idem*, OC, III, 506, *Plenitud de Plenitudes y Todo Plenitud!*

33. *Idem*, OC, IV, 704, *Del Sentimiento.*
34. *Idem*, OC, III, 1187, *Un Filósofo del Sentido Común.*
35. *Idem*, OC, IV, 812, *Alrededor del Estilo.*
36. *Idem*, OC, IV, 629, *Del Sentimiento.*
37. *Idem*, OC, III, 217, *La Ideocracia.*
38. *Idem*, OC, III, 1187, *Un Filósofo del Sentido Común.*
39. *Idem*, OC, IV, 773, *Alrededor del Estilo.*
40. *Idem*, OC, III, 1187, *Un Filósofo del Sentido Común.*
41. *Idem*, OC, III, 739, *Sobre la Consecuencia, la Sinceridad.*
42. *Idem*, OC, I, 87, *Recuerdos de Niñez y de Mocedad.*
43. *Idem*, OC, III, 461, *Intellectualidad y Espiritualidad.*
44. *Idem*, OC, IV, 368, *Vida de Don Quijote y Sancho.*
45. *Idem*, OC, IV, 723, *Aforismos y Definiciones.*
46. *Idem*, OC, III, 965, *Soliloquios y Conversaciones,* cf. the quotation from
O. W. Holmes' *The Autocrat of the Breakfast Table.*
47. *Idem*, OC, IV, 723, *Aforismos y Definiciones.*
48. *Idem*, OC, III, 1187, *Un Filósofo del Sentido Común.*
49. *Idem*, OC, IV, 724, *Aforismos y Definiciones.*
50. *Idem*, OC, III, 123, *La Enseñanza del Latín en España.*
51. *Idem*, OC, III, 573, *Sobre la Lectura e Interpretacion del "Quijote".*

Chapter 2

1. *Idem*, OC, II, 864, *Niebla.*
2. *Idem*, OC, IV, 533, *Del Sentimiento.*
3. *Idem*, OC, IV, 221, *Vida de Don Quijote y Sancho.*
4. *Idem*, OC, IV, 949, *Como Se Hace Una Novela.*
5. *Idem*, OC, IV, 206, *Vida de Don Quijote y Sancho.*
6. *Idem*, Menéndez y Pelayo, Palacio Valdés, *Epistolario a Clarín*, Prólogo y Notas de Adolfo Alas (Madrid: Ediciones Escorial, 1941), "Letter of May 10th, 1900," p. 103.
7. Unamuno, OC, III, 704, *Qué es Verdad?*
8. *Idem*, OC, III, 237, *La Fe.*
9. *Idem*, OC, III, 826, *Verdad y Vida.*
10. *Idem*, OC, III, 237, *La Fe.*
11. *Idem*, OC, IV, 206, *Vida de Don Quijote y Sancho.*
12. *Ibid.* We translated *creencia de verdad* as "genuine belief," and *lo es de mentira la que lleve* as "it is a pretense when it leads to;" the original is as follows: *Toda creencia que lleve a obras de vida es creencia de verdad, y lo es de mentira la que lleve a obras de muerte.*
13. *Idem*, OC, III, 222, *La Ideocracia.*
14. *Idem*, OC, IV, 612, *Del Sentimiento.*
15. *Idem*, OC, II, 984, *Tres Novelas Ejemplares y un Prólogo.*
16. *Idem*, OC, IV, 552, *Del Sentimiento.*
17. *Ibid.,* p. 614.
18. *Idem*, OC, II, 824, *Niebla.*
19. *Idem*, OC, IV, 617, *Del Sentimiento.*
20. *Idem*, OC, III, 222, *La Ideocracia.*
21. *Idem*, OC, IV, 331, *Vida de Don Quijote y Sancho.*
22. *Idem*, OC, III, 546, *Sobre la Soberbia.*
23. *Idem*, OC, III, 372, *Contra el purismo.*
24. *Idem*, OC, III, 947, *Escepticismo Fanático.*
25. *Idem*, OC, IV, 533, *Del Sentimiento.*

63

26. *Ibid.*, p. 617.
27. *Idem*, OC, IV, 829, *La Agonía del Cristianismo.*
28. *Idem*, OC, IV, 545, *Del Sentimiento.*
29. *Idem*, OC, III, 44, *En Torno al Casticismo.*
30. Evidence of this is circumstantial and based upon such affirmations as this: "the truth is something collective, social, even civil . . ." (OC, IV, 829, *La Agonía del Cristianismo*) ; "the order on which our society bases itself today, order which, as is known, is today the supreme criterion of the truth of any doctrine." (OC, IV, 209, *Vida de Don Quijote y Sancho*) ; and upon the description of the "psychical" men, or "intellectuals" in *Intellectualidad y Espiritualidad* (OC, III, 463).
31. *Idem*, OC, IV, 533, *Del Sentimiento.*
32. *Idem*, OC, III, 44, *En Torno al Casticismo.*
33. *Ibid.*, p. 10.
34. *Idem*, OC, IV, 545, *Del Sentimiento.*
35. *Ibid.*, p. 533.
36. *Ibid.*, p. 544.
37. *Ibid.*, p. 545.
38. *Ibid.*, p. 485.
39. *Idem*, OC, III, 8, *En Torno al Casticismo.*
40. *Ibid.* p. 9.
41. *Idem*, OC, IV, 617, *Del Sentimiento.*
42. *Idem*, OC, III, 45, *En Torno al Casticismo.*
43. *Idem*, OC, III, 700, *Qué es Verdad?*
44. *Idem*, OC, IV, 566, *Del Sentimiento.*

Chapter 3

1. Poincaré, H., *Science et Méthode* (Paris: Flammarion, 1908), pp. 50-3.
2. Unamuno, OC, III, 222, *La Ideocracia.*
3. *Idem*, OC, IV, 132, *Vida de Don Quijote y Sancho.*
4. *Idem*, OC, IV, 480, *Del Sentimiento.*
5. *Idem*, OC, IV, 255, *Vida de Don Quijote y Sancho.*
6. *Ibid.*, p. 206.
7. *Idem*, OC, I, 90, *Recuerdos de Niñez y de Mocedad.*
8. *Idem*, OC, IV, 533, *Del Sentimiento.*
9. *Idem*, OC, IV, 102, *Vida de Don Quijote y Sancho.*
10. *Ibid.*, p. 206.
11. *Idem*, OC, IV, 544, *Del Sentimiento.*
12. *Ibid.*, p. 534; cf. also III, 506, *Plenitud de Plenitudes y Todo Plenitud!*
13. *Idem*, OC, IV, 533, *Del Sentimiento.*
14. *Idem*, OC, III, ii, *En Torno al Casticismo.*
15. *Idem*, OC, IV, 548, *Del Sentimiento.*
16. *Idem*, OC, III, 120, *La Enseñanza del Latín en España.*
17. *Idem*, OC, IV, 533, *Del Sentimiento.*
18. *Ibid.*, p. 552.
19. *Idem*, OC, IV, 256, *Vida de Don Quijote y Sancho.*
20. *Ibid.*, p. 331.
21. *Idem*, OC, III, 249, *La Crisis del Patriotismo.*
22. *Idem*, OC, IV, 478-9, *Del Sentimiento.*
23. *Ibid.*, p. 472.
24. *Ibid.*, p. 544.
25. *Idem*, OC, IV, 206, *Vida de Don Quijote y Sancho.* (N. B. The word

"wanted" should be taken in its fully affective connotations and not merely intellectually.)

26. Cf. for example, E. Bréhier, "La Théorie des Incorporels dans l'Ancien Stoïcisme," *Archiv für Geschichte der Philosophie*, Bd XXII (Neue Folge XV Band) (Berlin: 1909), p. 120.

27. Unamuno, OC, III, 12, *En Torno al Casticismo.*

28. *Idem*, OC, IV, 232, *Vida de Don Quijote y Sancho.*

29. *Idem*, OC, IV, 949, *Como Se Hace una Novela.*

30. Antithetic pairings to this effect occur in various texts: OC, IV, 548, 601, *Del Sentimiento;* OC, IV, 331, 132, *Vida de Don Quijote y Sancho,* for example.

31. *Idem*, OC, III, 12, *En Torno al Casticismo.*

32. *Idem*, OC, IV, 533, *Del Sentimiento.*

33. *Ibid.*, p. 595.

34. *Ibid.*, p. 533.

35. *Idem*, OC, III, 409, *Sobre el Fulanismo,* a quotation from St. Augustine that Unamuno adopts.

36. *Idem*, OC, II, 985, *Tres Novelas Ejemplares.*

37. *Idem*, OC, III, 210-11, *Adentro!*

38. *Idem*, OC, IV, 491, *Del Sentimiento;* cf. also p. 331, *Vida de Don Quijote y Sancho.*

39. *Idem*, OC, IV, 552, *Del Sentimiento.*

40. *Idem*, OC, II, 984, *Tres Novelas Ejemplares.*

41. *Idem*, OC, IV, 552, *Del Sentimiento.*

42. *Ibid.*, p. 619.

43. *Idem*, OC, III, 799, *Sobre la Europeización.*

44. *Idem*, OC, IV, 548, *Del Sentimiento.*

45. *Idem*, OC, III, 12, *En Torno al Casticismo.*

46. *Idem*, OC, IV, 568, *Del Sentimiento.*

47. *Ibid.*, p. 567.

48. *Ibid.*, p. 569.

49. *Ibid.*, p. 570.

50. *Ibid.*, p. 481.

51. *Ibid.*, p. 569.

52. *Ibid.*, p. 573.

53. *Ibid.* N.B. "Sympathizes" is here taken in its etymological sense.

54. *Ibid.*, p. 619.

55. *Ibid.*, p. 626.

56. *Ibid.*, p. 552.

57. *Idem*, OC, III, 12, *En Torno al Casticismo.*

58. *Idem*, OC, IV, 620, *Del Sentimiento.*

59. *Idem*, OC, III, 1155, *Contra Esto y Aquello.*

60. *Idem*, OC, III, 461, *Intelectualidad y Espiritualidad.*

61. *Idem*, OC, III, 168, *El Caballero de la Triste Figura.*

62. *Idem*, OC, III, 45, *En Torno al Casticismo.*

63. *Idem*, OC, IV, 571, *Del Sentimiento.*

64. *Idem*, OC, IV, 312, *Vida de Don Quijote y Sancho.*

65. *Ibid.*, p. 371.

66. *Idem*, OC, III, 249, *La Crisis del Patriotismo.*

67. *Idem*, OC, III, 506, *Plenitud de Plenitudes y Todo Plenitud!*

68. *Idem*, OC, III, 76, *En Torno al Casticismo.*

69. *Idem*, OC, IV, 472, *Del Sentimiento.*

70. *Ibid.*, p. 462.

71. *Ibid.*, p. 472.

72. *Idem,* OC, III, 222, *La Ideocracia.*
73. *Idem,* OC, IV, 462, *Del Sentimiento.*
74. *Idem,* OC, III, 75, *En Torno al Casticismo.*
75. *Idem,* OC, IV, 462, *Del Sentimiento.*
76. *Idem,* OC, III, 506, *Plenitud de Plenitudes y Todo Plenitud!*
77. *Idem,* OC, IV, 704, *Del Sentimiento.*
78. *Idem,* OC, III, 4, *En Torno al Casticismo.*
79. *Idem,* OC, IV, 15, *Nicodemo el Fariseo.*
80. *Idem,* OC, IV, 478, *Del Sentimiento.*
81. *Idem,* OC, III, 507, *Plenitud de Plenitudes y Todo Plenitud!*
82. *Idem,* OC, IV, 87, *De la Enseñanza Superior en España.*

Chapter 4

1. *Idem,* OC, IV, 461, *Del Sentimiento.*
2. *Ibid.,* p. 462.
3. *Idem,* OC, IV, cf. pp. 206, 312, 371, *Vida de Don Quijote y Sancho,* for example.
4. *Ibid.,* p. 206.
5. *Idem,* OC, III, 44, *En Torno al Casticismo.*
6. *Idem,* OC, III, 496, *Sobre la Filosofía Española.*
7. *Ibid.,* p. 485.
8. *Idem,* OC, IV, 472, *Del Sentimiento.*
9. *Ibid.,* p. 462.
10. *Idem,* OC, III, 219, *La Ideocracia.*
11. *Idem,* OC, IV, 564, *Del Sentimiento.*
12. *Ibid.,* p. 463.
13. *Ibid.,* p. 483.
14. *Ibid.,* p. 549; from a quotation from Kierkegaard's *Unscientific Postscript,* chap. 3, endorsed by Unamuno.
15. *Ibid.,* p. 472.
16. *Ibid.,* p. 666.
17. *Idem,* OC, II, 341, *Amor y Pedagogía.*
18. *Idem,* OC, II, 73, *Paz en la Guerra.*
19. *Idem,* OC, I, 85-6, *Recuerdos de Niñez y de Mocedad.*
20. *Idem,* OC, II, 935, *Abel Sanchez.*
21. Plato, *Cratylus,* 440c, text and translation by H. N. Fowler, The Loeb Classical Library, (Boston: Harvard University Press, 1953), p. 190.
22. Unamuno, OC, IV, 486, *Del Sentimiento;* cf. also p. 484.
23. *Ibid.,* p. 572.
24. *Ibid.,* p. 474.
25. *Idem,* OC, III, 213, *Adentro.*
26. *Idem,* OC, IV, 371, *Vida de Don Quijote y Sancho.*
27. *Idem,* OC, IV, 565, *Del Sentimiento.*
28. *Ibid.,* p. 481.
29. Meyer, *op. cit.,* p. 3.
30. Unamuno, OC, III, 498, *Plenitud de Plenitudes y Todo Plenitud!* Rather than being meant here as a synonym of "synaesthesia," which is the English term corresponding to the Spanish one, Unamuno's usage is here somewhat different and led me to take the liberty to make a neologism. This term means the consciousness of the overall unity of our own sensations within one perceiving agent.
31. *Idem,* OC, IV, 489, *Del Sentimiento.*

32. *Ibid.*, p. 544.
33. *Ibid.*, p. 491.
34. *Ibid.*, p. 549, a quotation from Kierkegaard's *Unscientific Postscript*, chap. 3, endorsed by Unamuno.
35. *Ibid.*, p. 548.
36. *Ibid.*, p. 544. Unamuno here insists that reason only proves this "within its limits," and therefore not absolutely.
37. *Ibid.*, p. 556.
38. *Ibid.*, p. 471.
39. *Ibid.*, p. 487.
40. *Idem*, OC, IV, 379, *Vida de Don Quijote y Sancho.*
41. *Idem*, OC, IV, 559, *Del Sentimiento.*
42. *Ibid.*, p. 641.
43. *Ibid.*, p. 642.
44. *Ibid.*, p. 565.
45. *Ibid.*, p. 572.
46. *Ibid.*, p. 573.
47. *Ibid.*, p. 585.
48. *Idem*, OC, II, 1185, *San Manuel Bueno, Mártir.*
49. *Idem*, OC, IV, 548, *Del Sentimiento.*
50. *Idem*, OC, III, 412, *Sobre el Fulanismo.*
51. *Idem*, OC, I, 58, *Recuerdos de Niñez y Mocedad.*
52. *Idem*, OC, IV, 489, *Del Sentimiento.*
53. *Ibid.*, p. 550.
54. *Idem*, OC, IV, 208, *Vida de Don Quijote y Sancho.*
55. *Idem*, OC, IV, 958, *Como Se Hace una Novela.*
56. *Idem*, OC, IV, 573, *Del Sentimiento.*
57. *Idem*, OC, IV, 102, *Vida de Don Quijote y Sancho.*
58. *Idem*, OC, IV, 629, *Del Sentimiento.*
59. *Ibid.*, p. 572.
60. *Ibid.*, p. 643.
61. *Ibid.*, p. 619.
62. *Idem*, OC, IV, 102, *Vida de Don Quijote y Sancho.*
63. *Idem*, OC, III, 969, *Conversación Segunda.*
64. *Idem*, OC, III, 210-1, *Adentro.*
65. *Idem*, OC, IV, 727, *Aforismos.*
66. *Idem*, OC, IV, 467, *Del Sentimiento.*
67. *Ibid.*, p. 571.
68. *Idem*, OC, III, 265, *Civilización y Cultura.*
69. *Idem*, OC, III, 665, *Sobre el Rango y el Mérito.*
70. *Idem*, OC, I, 143, *Paisaje.*
71. *Idem*, OC, III, 507, *Plenitud de Plenitudes y Todo Plenitud!*
72. *Idem*, OC, IV, 15, *Nicodemo el Fariseo.*
73. *Idem*, OC, II, 693, *Niebla.*
74. *Idem*, OC, III, 222, *La Ideocracia.*
75. *Idem*, OC, IV, 585, *Del Sentimiento.*
76. *Idem*, OC, I, 143, *Paisaje.*
77. *Idem*, OC, IV, 470, *Del Sentimiento.*
78. *Idem*, OC, III, 610, *Soledad.*
79. *Idem*, OC, III, 170, *El Caballero de la Triste Figura.*
80. *Idem*, OC, IV, 208, *Vida de Don Quijote y Sancho.*
81. *Idem*, OC, II, 693, *Niebla.*
82. *Idem*, OC, IV, 705, *Del Sentimiento.*
83. *Ibid.*, p. 481.

84. *Idem*, "Palabra," *El Cristo de Velázquez*, poema (Buenos Aires: Espasa-Calpe Argentina) part IV, chap. III, p. 136.

85. *Idem*, OC, II, 848, *Niebla*.

86. *Idem*, OC, II, 321, *Paz en la Guerra*.

87. *Ibid.*, p. 322, seq.

88. *Ibid.*, p. 321.

89. *Idem*, OC, II, 1237, *San Manuel Bueno, Mártir*.

90. *Idem*, OC, IV, 644, *Del Sentimiento*.

91. *Idem*, OC, III, 17, *En Torno al Casticismo*.

92. *Idem*, OC, III, 793, *Sobre la Europeización*.

93. *Idem*, OC, IV, 621, *Del Sentimiento*.

94. *Idem*, OC, III, 268, *Civilización y Cultura*.

95. *Idem*, OC, IV, 435, *El Porvenir de España*.

96. *Idem*, OC, IV, 943, *Como Se Hace una Novela*.

97. *Idem*, OC, IV, 727, *Aforismos*.

98. *Idem*, OC, III, 266, *Civilización y Cultura*.

99. *Idem*, OC, II, 1229, *San Manuel Bueno, Mártir*.

100. Berkeley, G. *A Treatise Concerning the Principles of Human Knowledge*, sections 20 and 25, for example, in *The English Philosophers from Bacon to Mill*, E. A. Burtt, ed. (New York: The Modern Library, 1939), pp. 529-31, respectively.

101. Unamuno, OC, IV, 483, *Del Sentimiento*.

102. *Idem*, OC, II, 1300, *San Manuel Bueno, Mártir*.

103. *Idem*, OC, IV, 379, *Vida de Don Quijote y Sancho*.

104. *Idem*, OC, II, 1231, *San Manuel Bueno, Mártir*.

105. *Idem*, OC, II, 853, *Niebla*.

106. *Idem*, OC, IV, 15, *Nicodemo el Fariseo*.

107. *Idem*, OC, II, 981, *Tres Novelas Ejemplares*.

Chapter 5

1. *Idem*, OC, IV, 17, *Nicodemo el Fariseo*.

2. *Ibid.*, p. 27.

3. *Idem*, OC, III, 721, *El Secreto de la Vida*.

4. *Idem*, OC, III, 822, *Mi Religión*.

5. *Idem*, OC, IV, 544, *Del Sentimiento*.

6. *Ibid.*, p. 488.

7. *Idem*, OC, III, 12, *En Torno al Casticismo*.

8. *Idem*, OC, III, 613, *Soledad;* cf. also, IV, 203, *Vida de Don Quijote y Sancho*.

9. *Idem*, OC, IV, 616, *Del Sentimiento*.

10. *Ibid.*, p. 571.

11. *Ibid.*, p. 572.

12. *Idem*, OC, III, 209, *Adentro*.

13. *Idem*, OC, II, 981, *Tres Novelas Ejemplares*.

14. *Ibid.*, p. 982.

15. *Idem*, OC, IV, 620, *Del Sentimiento*.

16. *Idem*, OC, IV, 208, *Vida de Don Quijote y Sancho*.

17. *Idem*, OC, III, 222, *La Ideocracia*.

18. Marías, J., in *Filosofía Actual y Existencialismo*, p. 32, for example.

19. Unamuno, OC, IV, 550, *Del Sentimiento*.

20. *Idem*, OC, II, 982, *Tres Novelas Ejemplares*.

21. *Idem*, OC, III, 212, *Adentro*.

22. *Idem*, OC, IV, 102, *Vida de Don Quijote y Sancho*.
23. *Ibid.*, p. 275.
24. *Ibid.*, p. 208.
25. *Ibid.*, p. 135.
26. *Idem*, OC, IV, 469, *Del Sentimiento*.
27. *Ibid.*, p. 470.
28. *Ibid.*, p. 469.
29. *Ibid.*, p. 470.
30. *Ibid.*, p. 622.
31. *Ibid.*, p. 656.
32. *Idem*, OC, III, 821, *Mi Religión*.
33. *Idem*, OC, IV, 572, *Del Sentimiento*.
34. *Ibid.*, p. 626.
35. *Ibid.*, p. 630.
36. *Ibid.*, p. 573.
37. *Ibid.*, p. 599.
38. *Ibid.*, p. 604; *idem*, OC, IV, 831, *La Agonía del Cristianismo; idem*, OC, IV, 351, *Vida de Don Quijote y Sancho; idem*, OC, II, 853, *Niebla; idem*, OC, II, 1187, *San Manuel Bueno, Mártir*.
39. *Idem*, OC, IV, 763, *Alrededor del Estilo*.
40. *Idem*, OC, II, 847, seq., *Niebla*.
41. *Idem*, OC, IV, 596, *Del Sentimiento*.
42. *Ibid.*, p. 609; Unamuno mentions the text quoted as *Hebrews* 11:1, and though in the edition of his works quoted here the Greek text he quotes is inexact, the text it unmistakably copies, except for minor mistakes, is the following: "ἐλπιζομένον ὑπόστασις, πραγμάτων ἔλεγχος, οὐ βλεπομένων," *Novum Testamentum Graece* (Oxonii, MDCCCCI), p. 564.
43. *Idem*, OC, IV, 812, *Alrededor del Estilo*.
44. *Idem*, OC, IV, 29, *Nicodemo el Fariseo*.
45. *Idem*, OC, IV, 381, *Vida de Don Quijote y Sancho*.
46. *Idem*, OC, IV, 609, *Del Sentimiento*.
47. *Idem*, OC, III, 227, *La Fe*.
48. *Idem*, OC, IV, 595, *Del Sentimiento*.
49. *Ibid.*, p. 610.
50. *Ibid.*, p. 614.
51. *Idem*, OC, III, 237, *La Fe*.
52. *Ibid.*, p. 235.
53. *Idem*, OC, II, 864, *Niebla*.
54. *Idem*, OC, IV, 21, *Nicodemo el Fariseo*.
55. *Idem*, OC, IV, 391, *Vida de Don Quijote y Sancho*.
56. *Idem*, OC, IV, 621, *Del Sentimiento*.
57. *Idem*, OC, II, 983, *Tres Novelas Ejemplares*.
58. *Idem*, OC, IV, 620, *Del Sentimiento*.
59. *Idem*, OC, IV, 195, *Vida de Don Quijote y Sancho*.
60. *Idem*, OC, IV, 21, *Nicodemo el Fariseo*.
61. *Ibid.*, p. 24.
62. *Idem*, OC, IV, 492, *Del Sentimiento*.
63. *Ibid.*, pp. 666-7.
64. *Ibid.*, p. 645.
65. *Idem*, OC, II, 320, *Paz en la Guerra*.
66. *Idem*, OC, IV, 352, *Vida de Don Quijote y Sancho*.
67. Sénancour, E. de, "Letter XC," from *Obermann*, (Paris: G. Michaut, 1908): "Man is perishable. That may be; but let us perish resisting, and if nothingness is in store for us, let us not make it be justice."

68. Unamuno, OC, IV, 668, *Del Sentimiento.*
69. *Ibid.,* p. 681.
70. *Ibid.,* p. 682.
71. *Ibid.,* p. 642.
72. *Ibid.,* p. 679.
73. *Idem,* OC, IV, 797, *Alrededor del Estilo.*
74. *Idem,* OC, IV, 572, *Del Sentimiento.*
75. *Idem,* OC, IV, 136, *Vida de Don Quijote y Sancho.*
76. *Idem,* OC, III, 616, *Soledad.*
77. *Idem,* OC, III, 171, *El Caballero de la Triste Figura.*
78. *Idem,* OC, IV, 241, *Vida de Don Quijote y Sancho.*
79. *Ibid.,* p. 255.
80. *Ibid.,* p. 136.
81. *Ibid.,* p. 232.
82. *Idem,* OC, IV, 605, *Del Sentimiento.*
83. *Idem,* OC, IV, 118, *Vida de Don Quijote y Sancho.*

Date Due